God on Earth

"If you've got your bags packed and are ready to go and incarnate the gospel in this culture, think again. Better let the books in the Dialogue of Faith series rearrange what you take with you. Already this series has shown me my desperate need to unpack some baggage and repack for the challenges of tomorrow."

—LEONARD SWEET, author of *Out of the Question...Into the Mystery*

"Doug Banister takes us to some of the less-clear edges of the spiritual life, where many believers do not venture. And he can do this because he is clear that Christ is the Center. If your faith raises issues that are not often touched on in church, then read *God on Earth*. It will make you think. And hope!"

—LEIGHTON FORD, president of Leighton Ford Ministries

"Good essays offer a thoughtful writer's flashes of insight on one focused topic after another. *God on Earth* is the work of a good essayist, and this collection works like a night of watching fireworks."

—BRIAN MCLAREN, pastor and author of *A Generous Orthodoxy* and *The Church on the Other Side*

"Open this book and step inside a church that is true to Scripture, yet reconfigured for today's world. If you suspect there is more to church than the Sunday-morning production; if you are a Christian leader, tired of playing church; if you are a new Christian who wants an excellent introduction to church, then you must read this book."

—Chuck Smith, jr., pastor and author of *Epiphany: Discover the Delight of God's Word*

"*God on Earth* speaks to those of us who feel unconnected, disconnected, or misconnected to the church, but who nevertheless long for real spiritual connection. Packing great wisdom into plain talk, Doug Banister invites us to envision a genuine kind of community, a community of faith like Jesus intended for us to explore, share, and enjoy."

—STANLEY J. GRENZ, theologian and author of *Rediscovering the Triune God* and *A Primer on Postmodernism*

dialogue
of faith

GOD
ON EARTH

THE CHURCH—A HARD LOOK
AT THE REAL LIFE OF FAITH

by DOUGLAS BANISTER

WATERBROOK
PRESS

GOD ON EARTH
PUBLISHED BY WATERBROOK PRESS
2375 Telstar Drive, Suite 160
Colorado Springs, Colorado 80920
A division of Random House, Inc.

The author has made every effort to ensure the truthfulness of the stories and anecdotes in
this book. In a few instances, names and identifying details have been changed to protect
the privacy of the persons involved.

ISBN 1-57856-792-0

Copyright © 2005 by Douglas K. Banister

Published in association with the literary agency of Alive Communications, Inc., 7680
Goddard Street, Suite 200, Colorado Springs, Colorado 80920.

Library of Congress Cataloging-in-Publication Data
Banister, Doug, 1961–
God on earth : a hard look at the real life of faith / Doug Banister.
    p. cm.
  Includes bibliographical references.
  ISBN 1-57856-792-0
  1. Church. I. Title.
BV600.3.B375 2005
262—dc22   2004017408

Printed in the United States of America
2005—First Edition

10 9 8 7 6 5 4 3 2

For John Wood

CONTENTS

ACKNOWLEDGMENTS

The opportunity to write this book came at the perfect time in my life. Thank you, Glen Wagner and Chip MacGregor, for inviting me to spend two years thinking, praying, teaching, and talking about the church. And thank you, Father, for prompting them to think of me.

Some very special people have helped shape my thinking about the church. Thanks, first of all, to the good people of Fellowship Church. I learned much from you. Thanks, too, to the Friday breakfast and lunch groups and the Sunday Night Fellowship. You were, are, and continue to be the church to me in ways you'll never know. Thanks, also, to the New City Reading Group. You helped me find my voice. Special thanks as well to Kenny Woodhull and the New City Café and Mark Medley at the Trinity College of Ministry for providing many wonderful evenings of dialogue about the emerging church. Thanks, too, Leighton Ford. My love for the church is deeper because of our walks. And thanks to Ron Lee for demanding, insightful editing that helped the book mature.

Finally, thank you, Sandi, Bryden, Hunter, Sajen, Ashten, Tucker, and Misty. When I am with you, I taste the sweetness of community God wants us to enjoy in his church.

I'm from the first generation that really rejected modernity, rejected the notion that life had to be moving toward something," Jeff tells me between sips of coffee.

Jeff is a thoughtful, articulate, young health-care executive who is also a leader in his church. We're sitting in a corner booth of a downtown restaurant, and I've asked him to tell me why he chose to become part of a Christian faith community.

"Do you remember the book *Generation X*?" he asks. "My friends and I lived that way... a really fractured existence."

Jeff spent much of his twenties touring the country as a drummer for the band Hunting Sleeve. They cut an album, began to get some airplay, and even opened one night for Nirvana. But life on the road became grueling, lonely.

"I was living in the shadows, moving in dark things." That's how Jeff describes those days. So he decided to head back to graduate school to study literature.

"I was a storyteller," he recalls. "Life was about collecting stories."

He began writing a short story about "the deadening effect of unforgiveness." Jeff says, "It was about me as a ghost. That felt right. I'd completely lost my sense of self."

He became depressed and began seeing a therapist: "I dreaded living the next thirty years." He couldn't finish his degree. His dissertation on the loss of self in nihilistic literature pushed him deeper into despair, and writing about it haunted him. That's when Jeff fled a failed romantic relationship and moved to Knoxville, Tennessee.

"One night I felt like I was disappearing, and I prayed, *God, take my life; get me outta here.* I felt so dark. Then I heard: 'You are on the right track, but say it differently.' I knew it was Christ. So I prayed, *God take my life and use it.* I felt peace. The next morning I felt the Spirit come in and start cleaning out the darkness."

Jeff was wary of finding a church. "I'd done that before. I smoked pot with all the kids I went to church with. No thanks."

Eventually though, Jeff's hunger for spiritual community outweighed his fears of visiting a church. He opened a phone book, flipped to "Churches," and put his finger on one that was listed. He visited the next day, and he's still there.

"It felt safe," he recalls. "They said risky things there; they told the truth." He joined a small group of other Christians within the church. "In three weeks they knew me better than the friends I'd had for twenty-five years."

Jeff learned to forgive in this community of faith. He learned to be a leader. He began to rediscover his gifts as a teacher. And recently Jeff and his fiancée were married in his church.

"My community put on the wedding. They cooked the food. They served me... My friends had never seen anything quite like it... I've found people who really do love."

Still, life with other Christians is not without problems.

"You should know that I do struggle with church," Jeff adds, as if fearing he'd painted too rosy a picture. "It has a tendency to become an institution. There's such a difference between organic life and an institution."

Why are you reading a book about the Christian faith community? I'm guessing you have some level of interest in the church, either as a subject for examination and discussion or perhaps from personal experience. In fact, I'm guessing that you might identify with one of these three groups: the unconnected, the disconnected, or the misconnected.

The *unconnected* are those who aren't sure what people mean when they talk about "the church." They wonder if the pursuit of spirituality is an individual journey or if it's really more of a team sport. They're exploring different faith communities to see how church is done and if there might be a benefit in seeking partners on their spiritual journey. A quick flip through the phone book reveals hundreds of possibilities. Should they start with Wicca? How about Buddhism? Should they try visiting a Jewish temple or maybe a local Islamic mosque? Don't all religions basically lead to the same destination anyway?

If you're one of the unconnected, I hope this book will help you in your search for a spiritual home by explaining what Christians mean when we talk about the church. There is much that is good about every faith community, but they're not all the same. I trust that the time we spend together will help you understand what is distinctive about the Christian faith community and why so many people over the past two thousand years have chosen the church as their spiritual home.

If my description of the *unconnected* doesn't resonate with you, you may be one of the *disconnected.* You have encountered the church before, and the encounter wasn't pleasant. The word *church* brings up negative emotions for you. You may have a "God, save me from your followers" bumper sticker on your car. Yet you're willing to consider giving the church one last chance. Perhaps a friend you respect actually *likes* his or her church. Perhaps you noticed people from a church doing something good in your neighborhood. Perhaps you are drawn down pathways that have roots in ancient times and beliefs, something that's deep and enduring. Whatever the reason for your renewed interest in the church, you are reading this book for clarification. You're painfully aware of what the church *is*—a community of imperfect people. What you need is clarity about what the church has the potential to *become*—and what it *might already be* in some corners of the world.

If you are one of the disconnected, I hope this honest look at the church will encourage you to give it one more chance.

But maybe you're still thinking, *That's not me!* If so, perhaps you're one of the *misconnected*. You care about your church. You serve in your church. You enjoy most of the people there. You are the type of loyal, hard-working church member pastors love to mention in sermons. What your pastor doesn't know is that your love for your church is tinged with sadness. And what you don't know is that your pastor probably feels the same. You both have a dream of what the church could be, but in the stark light of reality, the dream haunts you.

If you are one of the misconnected, I hope this book will inspire you with a fresh vision for the church. I hope you will become more grateful for the church you are a part of and hungrier for the church you dream of.

I write as a wounded lover of the church. For several years on Monday nights, I used to put on an apron and food-handling gloves so I could take my place as the dessert man at the Knoxville Area Rescue Mission. Have you ever wondered what happens to packaged baked goods when the best-used-by date passes? We'd get them at the mission. Homeless people don't care much about expiration dates. Life for them expired a long time ago. One week in mid-January, assorted Christmas pastries crowded my serving table. Sam's chocolate muffins were big that night. So was two-week-old apple pie.

"One thing about Knoxville," Elmo, one of our regulars, told me. "A man is not going to go hungry in this town."

It wasn't always that way.

Cormac McCarthy wrote about Knoxville's homeless in his gloomy novel *Suttree*. Suttree, a homeless man living in a dilapidated houseboat on the Tennessee River in the 1950s, must catch carp to sell if he has any hope of buying a meal. No carp, no food. His friend Harrogate has stooped even lower.

Harrogate watching the gutters for anything edible fallen from the trucks. By the time he reached the end of the street he had a small bouquet of frazzled greenstuffs and a washed tomato. He went into the markethouse and washed these things at the drinking fountain marked White and ate them while he wandered down the vast hall with its rich reek of meat and produce.... Harrogate went by, chewing his lettuce.... A family of trashpickers was packing flat cartons onto a child's wagon, the children scurrying along the rancid cans like rats and as graylooking. None spoke…the children made forays into trashbins and cellar doors, watching Harrogate all the while.[1]

Children don't rummage through trash bins for food in Knoxville today because the people in Knoxville's churches decided it wasn't right. Churches of various denominations and ethnicities all came together to help.

I love the church because the church feeds my friend Elmo.

Terry, a busy professional who began attending our church after a series of bad church experiences, called me late one night several years ago. "Does God really love me like you talked about last Sunday?" His voice had a note of desperation in it, as if he had asked this question many times before. We met the next day, and it wasn't long before I realized Terry was one of life's winners: pretty wife, great kids, plenty of money, and a high-profile career that kept him in demand across the nation. Yet Terry's inner life was in ruins. He was tormented with guilt. He was certain God was never pleased with him. And he was angry. Terry's inner world was quietly self-destructing.

Terry recognized the impending disaster and decided to do one thing differently. He began to do life with a handful of men who came together each week to pray, study the scriptures, tell an occasional joke, and talk about their lives. Several years into these relationships, Terry felt safe enough to reveal some of the darker corners of his inner world. The men around him didn't try to fix Terry, and they refused to judge him. Instead, they listened, did things together, and revealed their own dark corners. Seven years later these men are still doing life together. Terry doesn't call me anymore asking if God loves him. He knows. He's experienced God's love in the spiritual community he's chosen to walk out life with. The demons that once haunted him are mostly gone.

God used a handful of people following Christ together—as good a definition of the church as I've found—to help Terry answer his question. Yes, God loves you. He loves you through the people you go through life with.

I love the church because the church helped Terry.

Say what you want about the church, but the mundane rhythms of church life nurture friendship in a world that is more disconnected with each passing day. I have no trouble casting my vote with connections in an increasingly fragmented world. The friends who sat with us while we waited to find out how far the cancer had spread; the friends who made a video for my fortieth birthday, featuring interviews with a dozen people about my first book, which none of them had ever heard of; the friend who chopped firewood for me when I was visiting my mother-in-law in an Alzheimer's ward; the friends I gathered for support and input during a career transition, who didn't listen very well but loved me anyway. These friendships came to me through my church.

I love the church because the church has helped me.

I've also been wounded by the church. Not often. Not bad enough to wipe me out. But enough to know that people who come together to follow God inevitably hurt one another. So I write as a realist, living in the tension between what is and what might be. And in the conversation that follows, I will try to strike a balance between hope and honesty.

Each of the following essays can be read in fifteen minutes or less and in any order. Let your intuition—an important ingredient in spiritual growth—guide you. Search the table of contents, see which essays interest you, and start there. Don't worry about reading every essay.

Imagine that you and I are at Starbucks sipping lattes and talking about church. You set the pace, ask the questions, and end our conversation when you have what you need. Get mad. Disagree. Say nasty things. Compliment me a time or two. We'll both be better for it when we're through.

Conversations are reciprocal. I'm going to begin the conversation by describing what I think the church is. The last essay in this book asks you to put into your own words what you believe about the church. You may want to take some notes along the way as you come up with your own definition, or you may choose to talk with a friend about the kind of church you dream about. Either way, you get the last word.

PRAGUE, 1989

Václav Havel had had enough. A brilliant son of wealthy parents who lost their fortune when the Communists took over Czechoslovakia in 1948, Havel was banned from higher education and forced to support himself by working in a brewery. Communist oppression could not, however, silence his pen. In 1963 Havel wrote *The Garden Party*, a defiant protest against totalitarianism that led to the famous Prague Spring, when thousands of young Czechs tried to revolt against Communist rule only to be crushed by Soviet tanks. Havel found himself in jail for his troubles.

A decade passed. Havel continued writing letters, plays, and essays that were published secretly throughout Czechoslovakia. Intellectuals began to wrestle with the quiet questions of revolutionaries: "How can we live in a culture based on a lie? How can we ever hope again? Will things ever change?"

Havel's own answer came in 1978 when he secretly published his famous essay "The Power of the Powerless." He called for the creation of parallel communities where "a different life can be lived...within the truth." The parallel communities would be a "non-violent attempt by people to negate the system within themselves and to establish their lives on a new basis."[1]

Soon, small groups of people eager to live in the truth began to meet secretly. They read Plato. They put on plays. They performed music. They danced. They created parallel communities, alternative worlds in which people lived and spoke and danced the truth. Gradually the groups spread. Truth replaced lies. Hope was renewed. The system trembled.

This movement mirrored something that occurred in ancient times. The biblical writers, quiet revolutionaries in their own way, also referred to the world we live in as a dark, oppressive system that uses deception and lies to crush the spirits of good people. The world into which Jesus was born is described as "the darkness," and those who live in the darkness live a "lie."[2] Satan, the ruler of this oppressive system, is "the father of lies" whose work is to deceive.[3]

Think of some of the lies that oppress us:

- consumerism—the lie that you are what you buy
- racism—the lie that one race is superior to another
- sexism—the lie that one gender is better than the other
- materialism—the lie that what you see is all there is
- hedonism—the lie that pleasure can dull the ache in our hearts
- pessimism—the lie that there is no hope
- nationalism—the lie that one nation is better or more blessed by God than any other nation in the world
- narcissism—the lie that I am the center of the universe, that my needs and desires take priority over yours, and that every other being, whether plant, animal, or human, exists for my benefit alone

What is God's plan for subverting the world system that is based on lies so that he can establish a liberating reign of truth? Parallel communities, very similar to the kind Václav Havel brought about.

The first eleven chapters of the first book of the bible record the rise and fall of a great planet. The world, plunged into sin by the first couple's rebellion against God, grows progressively darker. The perceptive reader of that narrative wonders what God will do to turn back the darkness.

Enter stage right, a shriveled old man named Abram and his barren wife, Sarai. "I will make you into a great nation…," God promises the tired couple. "All peoples on earth will be blessed through you."[4] Sarai laughs, shaking her gray head in disbelief. At Sarai's urging, Abram takes matters into his own hands and makes a mess of things. Finally, God allows the aged lovers to give birth to a son named Isaac, from whom the nation of Israel will emerge. (The whole story is found in chapters 12 through 25 of Genesis. It's a great read.)

This is a strange way to save the world. God creates from one elderly couple a nation of people who will live as a parallel community among all the other nations of the earth. Within their own community they will learn and dance and sing the truth. Even better, all nations on earth will be blessed as a result of this parallel community.

The first five books of the Old Testament, commonly known as the Torah, describe the birth of this parallel community called Israel. The people of Israel are to live by an alternative vision. They are to model God's character. Israel, when she lives according to this alternative vision, will "show [her] wisdom and understanding to the nations" and become a "light for the Gentiles [all non-Jewish people]."[5]

Jesus enters the picture a few thousand years later to give maximum expression to the parallel faith community. He does not introduce Plan B. He continues building the parallel community first conceived in Sarah's womb. He begins by forming a very small parallel community made up of twelve men, his closest disciples. The Jews of the first century, who found deep significance in certain numbers, no doubt grasped what Jesus was trying to say. Just as the parallel community of Israel had twelve tribes, so the parallel community of the new Israel will be formed around twelve disciples.

Much earlier Moses had shaped the life of the parallel community by bringing the law from the mountain. In the first century Jesus shapes the life of the parallel community by instructing them in the law in his famous Sermon on the Mount. Israel, the Old Testament parallel community, was called to be a light to the Gentiles. The new Israel, which is the parallel community of the New Testament, is to be "the light of the world."[6] Moses called Israel "a kingdom of priests."[7] A priest is a mediator, an intercessor, a bridge-builder between God and people. Israel was to mediate between God and the people around her. She was to build a redemptive bridge over which her neighbors could find the way back to God. Peter, one of Jesus's closest followers, echoes this language when he reminds the churches scattered throughout the Roman Empire, "You are…a royal priesthood."[8]

Peter also echoes the language of the parallel community, making it clear that God's people are to be distinct from the darkness of the world's system. He describes those in the Christian faith community "as aliens and strangers in the world" and challenges them to live in such a truthful way that their neighbors "may see [their] good deeds and glorify God."[9]

The New Testament calls this parallel community "the church," which literally means "called-out ones." God calls people into this community made up of "aliens," foreigners, expatriates—people with different passports who don't call this world home. The church is a colony of people with citizenship in another kingdom, a spiritual one.

Although the church belongs to another world, she is still fully present and warmly engaged with her neighbors in this world. A friend of mine, Shelly Kreykes, after participating in a discussion on the tension between the parallel community of the first century and the world system of that time, e-mailed me these thoughts:

> The "otherness" or "peculiarity" or "set apartness" they [the first-century faith community] displayed uniquely released them to move deeply into their culture. The simple living of their lives was their apologetic; their lives *spoke*.[10]

This is a necessary and distinctive trait of the parallel faith community—the life that stands out and at times stands apart from the surrounding culture. The church is "other," apart from the world system. But the church is also engaged in the culture. Some writers have tried to resolve this tension by describing the church as an alternative community or a counterculture. But these terms push the church too far away from the world. Havel's term "parallel culture" captures the tension better. The church is a colony of expatriates whose citizenship is in another kingdom. But the church exists parallel to her neighbors, not removed from them. Even though the church is a radically different kind of community, she is nonetheless a community very much involved with her neighbors by caring, loving, serving, and being living representatives of Christ to them.

On November 17, 1989, fifty thousand Czechs filled the streets of Prague in a student-led protest demanding freedom. The numbers swelled to three-quarters of a million people in the protests of November 25 and 26. The secret police, riot police, and Interior Ministry troops waited in vain for orders to assault the protesters. The orders never came. On December 3 the Soviet Union and the Warsaw Pact issued separate statements condemning the Soviet invasion of Czechoslovakia in 1968. By the end of December 1989, Václav Havel, the most articulate and outspoken opponent of the Soviet regime, had become president of the same nation that had once imprisoned him.

The transfer of power was dubbed the "Velvet Revolution." The parallel communities had done their subversive yet bloodless work: They had lived the truth amidst the lie, and they brought down the system.

The parallel communities of the early church had a staggering impact on their world as well. These colonies of believers lived out an alternative vision that was so appealing that many of their neighbors joined the Christian community. The Roman emperor Julian is one of many who noted the strange power of these tiny colonies. The church "has been specially advanced through the loving service rendered to strangers," he fumed. "The godless Galileans care not only for their own poor but for ours as well."[11]

What might a parallel faith community look like today? Duke University's Will Willimon gives us a good idea. The parallel community of the church, he writes, is "a place, clearly visible to the world, in which people are faithful to their promises, love their enemies, tell the truth, honor the poor, suffer for righteousness, and thereby testify to the amazing community-creating power of God."[12]

Faithfulness, love, truth, compassion, righteousness, power. The most persuasive argument for the validity and value of the church is the life of this parallel community when it is lived faithfully in contrast to the world's system.

THE HOMECOMING OF GOD

I spent the night once with a dozen heroin addicts outside a bus station in Rome. During my flight home from a teaching assignment in Eastern Europe, I had a lay over at Leonardo da Vinci Airport, which left me with a free evening in one of the world's great cities. I converted my remaining traveler's checks into Italian lire and bought a token on the first subway train I could find. An hour later I bought another token and got on a train that actually went *toward* Rome. I finally emerged from the underground station a few blocks from the Coliseum a bit after ten o'clock. Quite a bit after ten.

Cheap tourist map firmly in hand, I began my late-night walking tour. I walked past the Coliseum. I walked past the Vatican. I walked past the Spanish Steps and St. Peter's basilica. I walked past lots of old things that would, if they were in the United States, be torn down to make space for a Wal-Mart or a Home Depot. Then I walked back to the subway to go home, but the subway was closed. Taxis sped past with signs posted in their windows that, roughly translated, said, "You're crazy if you think I'm going to stop for you." One driver finally did stop, saying he'd take me to my hotel for sixty dollars American. I didn't have that much, so I joined the heroin addicts at the bus station, hoping the subway would be running in time for me to get my bags from the hotel so I could catch the plane home.

Rome offers her guests a gift that American cities cannot give: a taste of life as it was lived in the ancient past. Walk the streets for an hour with just a dash of imagination, and you can hear and see the Rome of the first century—togas, gladiators, chariots, and everything else. What struck me about the ancient Rome I observed on my midnight walk was its throbbing spirituality. If architecture reveals anything about the soul of a city, Rome's ruins reveal a community aching for God. Reminders of ancient temples are everywhere. Climb to the top of Palatine Hill, and you discover well-preserved samples of Roman temples and palaces where the prayers of thousands once were heard. Wander the grounds of the Roman Forum, and you notice the temple ruins resting quietly in the shadows. You can imagine the hundreds of virgins who once guarded the sacred fires in the Temple of Vesta. You can almost hear the prayers of the long dead whispering in the wind.

Every city of the first-century Roman Empire was a religious city, dotted with temples. "The standard Roman city," writes Yale historian Ramsay MacMullen, "would need temples to the Capitoline Triad [Jupiter, Juno, and Minerva], plus Mercury, Isis and Sarapis, Apollo, Liber Pater, Hercules, Mars, Venus, Vulcan and Ceres."[1] A god or goddess lived in a temple. Worshipers came to the temple to be in the presence of their god.

In the early church, followers of Jesus wondered where their temple would be. Where would their God dwell? Where would they find his presence? Steeped as they were in the Hebrew scriptures, the early Christians knew that their God desired to dwell with his people. In fact, the story of God seeking ways to live among his people is one of the main plots running through the entire bible. And it's easily one of the most compelling of all the biblical plot lines.

Here's a major plot line from the biblical narrative: The people of God, held as slaves in Egypt for four hundred years, are liberated by Moses—the Martin Luther King, Jr., of their day. God leads them through the deserts of Sinai and prepares them for life in "the promised land," a piece of waterfront property sandwiched between the Mediterranean Sea and the Dead Sea. The land of promise is one hundred twenty miles long and forty miles wide. God pledges to go with his people into their new homeland and commands them to "make a sanctuary [temple] for me."[2] We find the blueprint for God's dream home in the final chapters of the book of Exodus. It will be beautiful, made by the finest craftsmen, and it will be portable so that it can be carried by the community as they travel through the desert. When this portable temple is completed, God moves in.[3]

We get a glimpse of how desperate the people were for the presence of God as we read the passionate prayer of Moses, offered in a moment when the people's sins appeared to have alienated God's affections:

> If your Presence does not go with us, do not send us up from
> here. How will anyone know that you are pleased with me and
> with your people unless you go with us? What else will distinguish
> me and your people from all the other people on the face of the
> earth?[4]

Years later, after the people of Israel had settled in the promised land, King Solomon builds God a magnificent temple to take the place of the portable tabernacle. God "moves in" again, but tragically he does not stay. Solomon's sons allow the kingdom to split into two self-governing territories. The northern kingdom and the southern kingdom slaughter each other in horrific battles. Eventually, God gets fed up. In a cryptic passage from the strange book of Ezekiel, the prophet shares a vision of God's presence packing up and moving out: "The glory of the LORD departed from over the threshold of the temple."[5] God no longer lives there, and the community experiences what Moses feared most: God's absence.

Israel's prophets lament God's departure with the anguish of a lover who mourns the death of a spouse. And yet there is promise mingled with their grief. God says he will dwell once again with his people.[6] The final pages of the Old Testament are filled with longing for God's home-coming. But *when* would he come and fill his temple again?

Near the beginning of the New Testament, Jesus gathers a community and pledges to remain present within it through the Holy Spirit. After thirty-three years of life on the earth, Jesus dies, is raised from the dead, and returns to heaven. Then, on the Day of Pentecost, the church receives God's promise of the Holy Spirit.

The plot thickens in AD 70 when Roman soldiers raid Jerusalem and destroy the Jewish temple. Now where would God dwell? Everyone had thought he would return to the temple, but now it has been reduced to ruins. Every other religion has a temple for its gods. Where would the temple of the living God be?

The apostle Paul, writing after Jesus's death, resurrection, and return to heaven, surprises the church with his answer. The temple, he notes in a letter to believers living in Ephesus, is *you*. "You are...built on the foundation of the apostles and prophets, with Christ Jesus himself as the chief cornerstone." Continuing with the metaphor of a physical temple, he adds: "In him the whole building is joined together and rises to become *a holy temple* in the Lord."[7]

You won't find the new temple in Jerusalem or on a hill outside Rome. It is not made of bricks or stone. You find the temple of the Christian God wherever his people come together. As Paul words it: "In him you too are being built together to become a dwelling in which God lives by his Spirit."[8] God dwells within the gathered faith community.[9]

The biographer of the great British preacher D. Martyn Lloyd-Jones tells the story of a well-known London witch who converted to Christianity after attending Westminster Chapel, Lloyd-Jones's church: "The moment I entered your chapel and sat down on a seat amongst the people, I was conscious of a supernatural power," the woman recalled. "I was conscious of the same sort of supernatural power as I was accustomed to in our spiritist meetings, but there was one big difference; I had the feeling that the power in your chapel was a clean power."[10] The proof of God's existence is not a rational argument; it is nothing less than the experience of God's presence in the midst of his people. God's presence touches all of us in ways arguments can't.

Harvard theologian Harvey Cox became famous thirty years ago by proclaiming the imminent death of religion in the coming "post religious age." Now, he sees things quite differently. His book *Fire from Heaven* talks about Pentecostalism and its vitality in a world that longs to encounter God. Cox recalls attending a Pentecostal rally during his freshman year of college. He and another young intellectual went "to see the show." Cox remembers that afterward "we walked to his [the friend's] trolley stop without saying anything, and as he climbed on board I just said, 'Really something, eh, Bill?' 'Yeah,' he answered, still staring ahead as the trolley pulled away. I could sense that although we had come mainly out of curiosity, maybe even to be entertained, we had found ourselves in the presence of something that was more than we expected."[11]

They hadn't expected to encounter the presence of God.

SACRED CONVERSATIONS

One steamy June night in 2001, I left the kibbutz where I was staying on the Sea of Galilee and took a walk along the beach. The modern streetlights of ancient Tiberias flickering across the lake were the only reminder that nearly two thousand years had passed since Jesus walked these same shores.

I'm not a very mystical person. I don't see visions or hear audible voices. God usually speaks to me internally, in his still, small voice. This night, however, was different. Perhaps it was the cumulative effect of three dusty weeks wandering the holy places of Israel. Perhaps it was the magic of ancient breezes sweeping down from the Golan Heights, bearing secrets of sacred pasts. Perhaps it was the need I had for a simple encounter with Jesus after many hours of hearing lectures about holy sites. Whatever the cause, Jesus joined me on my walk. Or perhaps I joined him. Two millennia slipped beneath the dark waves, and I found myself half-imagining and half-seeing a scene from the gospel of Mark: "As Jesus walked beside the Sea of Galilee, he saw Simon and his brother Andrew casting a net into the lake, for they were fishermen. 'Come, follow me,' Jesus said."[1]

I sensed Jesus saying to me, "This is what it means to be a Christian. This is what it means to be part of my church." Then the encounter was over, and I was alone again on the beach.

Since that night I've thought many times about that simple vision of

Jesus inviting Simon and Andrew to follow him. Being a Christian means following Jesus Christ. The church is a community of people who have chosen to follow him together. Forming a community was Jesus's first act when he began his ministry. "Jesus went up on a mountainside and called to him those he wanted…," Mark wrote. "He appointed twelve…that they might be with him."[2]

The community would "be with him" in intimate, conversational relationship for three wonderful, terrifying years. They would rarely be apart. Jesus, the master teacher, would use every conceivable opportunity to shape them into a community. He taught them. He corrected them. He warned them. He listened to their questions. He challenged them. He protected them. Most of all, he guided them.

When the original twelve disciples said yes to Jesus, they also said yes to life in a conversational community. They would learn to hang on every word their master spoke. His words became life to them. Jesus, whom one of the disciples would later describe as "the Word,"[3] was in continual conversation with his community, preparing them for the task ahead, shaping them into the kind of parallel community that would bless the world.

The final hours of Jesus's life on earth find him, not surprisingly, in conversation with his community. It is Thursday night. The streets of Jerusalem are crowded with dusty pilgrims arriving to celebrate Passover, an annual observance that commemorates God's miraculous act of freeing the Hebrew slaves from Egypt. The joyous sounds of festival, of laughter and greetings and preparation, fill the street outside the upstairs room where the community sits. The mood inside the room is not joyous, however. Jesus is somber as he prepares them for his death.

Jesus comforts his community of twelve with a promise of continued conversation. "I will not leave you as orphans…," he begins, noting the fear in their eyes. "The Counselor, the Holy Spirit, whom the Father will send in my name, will teach you all things and will remind you of everything I have said to you."[4] He spends a few moments preparing them for what is to come and then returns to his comforting promise of continued personal conversation. "But when he, the Spirit of truth, comes," Jesus says gently, "he will guide you into all truth…. The Spirit will take from what is mine and make it known to you."[5]

Jesus is arrested later than night. The next day he is crucified. Then, three days later, he is raised from the dead.

Brought back to life, he calls together the community for a conversation. They meet on a favorite hillside in Galilee where they talked many times before. Jesus instructs the community to go out into the world and invite others to become followers of Jesus. He adds: "I am with you always, to the very end of the age."[6] The conversation will continue.

Forty days pass. Jesus gathers the community on the Mount of Olives, just outside Jerusalem. He gives them their mission one final time before he returns to heaven, commanding them to stay put until he sends them the gift of the Holy Spirit. They wait. Then on Pentecost, the great Jewish festival celebrated on the fiftieth day after Passover, Jesus keeps his word and pours out the Holy Spirit on his followers.[7]

And the conversation between Jesus and his community continues to our own day.

DARING TO SPEAK FOR GOD

Bill fell asleep one Sunday morning while I was preaching. Bill snores—loudly. I laughed so hard I never finished the sermon. Then there was the time I fell down as I approached the pulpit. Sprawled-out-on-the-carpet down.

Preaching can be humbling. What are people like me doing, anyway, daring to speak for God?

On Saturday nights before I preach, I pace my study, wondering whether God will speak through me the next day. Often I turn to a dog-eared, yellow-highlighted page in Frederick Buechner's classic, *Telling the Truth,* to remind me why we preach.

Fresh from breakfast with his wife and children and a quick run-through of the Sunday papers, the preacher climbs the steps to the pulpit with his sermon in his hand. He hikes his black robe up at the knee so he will not trip over it on the way up. His mouth is a little dry. He has cut himself shaving. He feels as if he has swallowed an anchor. If it weren't for the honor of the thing, he would just as soon be somewhere else.... The vice-president of a bank who twice that week has seriously contemplated suicide places his hymnal in the rack. A pregnant girl feels the life stir inside her. A high-school math teacher, who for twenty years has managed to keep his homosexuality a secret for the most part even from himself, creases his order of service down the center with his thumbnail and tucks it under his knee. [Another preacher] is there. The vestry has urged him to take a week off for a badly needed rest, and he has come to hear how somebody else does it for a change.…

The preacher pulls the little cord that turns on the lectern light and deals out his note cards like a riverboat gambler. The stakes have never been higher.[1]

The church preaches because Jesus has something he wants to say to the suicidal bank president, the pregnant girl, the homosexual high-school teacher, and the visiting, burned-out minister. The cry of the prophets to ancient Israel was, "Come here and listen to the words of the LORD your God."[2] This is why the church hears a sermon every week: to listen to the words of God.

Shortly after his resurrection, Jesus joined two of his discouraged disciples on a dusty road, and "beginning with Moses and all the Prophets, he explained to them what was said in all the Scriptures concerning himself."[3] A sermon is not just a lecture about a sacred book. Jesus, the Living Word, reveals *himself* to his community in the sermon event.

But how can this be? What right do we have to expect to meet the Living Word himself through the plain words of a preacher who just that morning cut himself shaving?

Our hope for an encounter with the Living Word rests first in the character of the words of scripture. The church believes that the words of scripture are divinely inspired: God's voice is somehow hidden within the hundreds of thousands of words found in the pages of the bible. The Living Word somehow dwells within the written word.

Our hope for a roadside encounter with Jesus rests second on the ministry of the Holy Spirit. Either Jesus honors his long-ago promise to keep talking to us or he doesn't. If he is keeping his promise, then the Spirit is still carrying on our conversation with Jesus. Mysteriously this conversation continues through the sermon, where the preacher—who has struggled all week with his own lusts, fears, and failures—nonetheless preaches in the desperate hope that the Spirit will breathe on his words and bring them alive and kicking into the haunted places of the congregation. That is the mystery and miracle of preaching.

It's good to recognize, however, that not all preaching takes place from behind a lectern. Some church watchers worry aloud about "a pastor-dominated, sermon-driven worship machine that actually hinders the average player's role in Kingdom expansion."[4] Facing head-on the unarguable reality that people learn better when they interact with the subject matter instead of passively listening, churches are experimenting with new ways to make preaching more interactive. I know of a house church in Huntsville, Alabama, where different members preach from the scriptures each week, sometimes spontaneously, sometimes after long and careful preparation.

There is more than one way to dare to speak for God.

PRAYER

Visit any Christian faith community in the world, and you will find people who pray. If you are not at a point on the spiritual journey where you pray when you're alone, you will at least be around people who do.

You might kneel and say the Lord's Prayer:

Our Father in heaven,
hallowed be your name,
your kingdom come,
your will be done
      on earth as it is in heaven.
Give us today our daily bread.
Forgive us our debts,
      as we also have forgiven our debtors.
And lead us not into temptation,
but deliver us from the evil one.[1]

Or after a moment of silence, a young woman wearing a black robe with a white collar and a silver cross hung loosely around her neck might step onto the stage. She quietly takes a note card from her bible, places it before her on the lectern, and starts to pray. She prays for the sick. She prays for the dying. She prays for marriages and children. She prays for the hungry, the poor, and the oppressed. She prays for peace. And she prays for Christ's presence to grace the rest of the church service. And then she says "Amen."

Or the congregation's worship leader, a thirtyish-looking man with a shaved head, earring, faded jeans, and scuffed Birkenstocks might stop and set aside his guitar. "Tonight we want you to pray with the people at your table," he says, looking out over a group gathered in a former warehouse. Several hundred people are sitting at tables, drinking coffee. "Check in with each other and then spend some time praying for each other."

Or a dozen friends might gather in an apartment on a Thursday night. They've been listening to a live recording of a huge worship gathering. Actually, "listening" isn't the right word. These twelve are engaged, passionately, with what they are experiencing. Some stand, hands lifted in the air. Some lie on the floor, facedown in the carpet. Others sit quietly on couches and chairs. As the CD nears its final song, time and space are transcended. The dozen friends are swept away by a worship experience much larger than themselves. They have fallen into a swiftly moving spiritual current that is taking them places they've never dreamed of going. The final song ends. There is silence.

Following the silence there is a word, many words, a river of words, words of praise and beauty, words in a heavenly language that pour from the mouth of a young woman sandwiched on the couch between two friends. More silence. Then, another prayer from another mouth.

Or you might be present with monks who listen for the bell that signals the night office—a time of prayer. Benedictine monks file silently into the darkness of a cathedral. They line up, facing one another in two rows, preparing to address the God who waits for them beyond the silence of the still night.

"Praise the LORD, O my soul; all my inmost being, praise his holy name," chant the monks on the left. They are praying the Psalms, the one hundred fifty prayers and hymns that Jews and Christians have been praying for three thousand years. "Praise the LORD, O my soul, and forget not all his benefits," chant the monks on the right, praying as their brothers before them have prayed every night since Saint Benedict founded this religious order in the sixth century.[2]

The Holy Spirit who fills the church with the speaking Christ is himself a speaker. "The Spirit himself intercedes for us with groans that words cannot express."[3] This Spirit-inspired speaking is called prayer.

God's people are lovers who are overwhelmed by the beauty and kindness of the One they love, so they recite and sing and pray prayers of praise and worship and adoration and thanks to God. The writer of the book of Hebrews calls the church to "continually offer to God a sacrifice of praise."[4] One kind of prayer is loving God and telling him that you love him.

Another kind of prayer is known as intercessory prayer in which members of the universal family of God pray for their brothers and sisters when they are in need. The apostle Paul almost always began his letters with a heartfelt prayer for the people he was writing to. Prayers for the well-being of others rise up in Paul's letters almost unconsciously, so deeply rooted was he in the ancient discipline of intercessory prayer. Tucked away in the final chapters of his letter to the Romans, in a portion of the letter where the apostle was tidying up a lot of loose ends, is a prayer he managed to sneak in: "May the God who gives endurance and encouragement give you a spirit of unity."[5] In the church we find this kind of conversation with God occurring naturally, spontaneously, and instantaneously as part of our common life.

God's people pray for one another at meals, while working out at the gym, over the cell phone, via e-mail. It's as natural as talking about the weather. We love one another. We pray for one another.

And God's people pray for those outside God's family, as Jesus instructed. In the Lord's Prayer, Jesus summoned his followers to pray for

God's kingdom to come on earth as it exists in heaven. So today we continue to pray that the peace of the next world might break into the pain of our own world. We pray that God will bless our nation, but we don't stop there, because God is not an American God. We ask God to bless the people of Iraq and North Korea and Israel and Afghanistan and every other nation. We pray for the AIDS crisis in Africa, even as we build hospices and send medicine. We pray for the orphans and widows in Vietnam, even as we support orphanages. We love the world. We pray for the world.

When someone speaks to you, the polite response is to say something in return. We speak in prayer because God speaks to us. He started it.

STOLEN GLOVES

Charles Spurgeon was the most popular British preacher of the nineteenth century. Once, while giving a sermon at Exeter Hall, Spurgeon stopped and pointed at a man in the audience. "Young man," he said, "those gloves you are wearing have not been paid for. You have stolen them from your employer." Afterward the man confessed that he had indeed stolen the gloves and would make restitution.

In his autobiography, Spurgeon reflected on incidents such as this one:

I could tell as many as a dozen similar cases in which I pointed at somebody in the hall without having the slightest knowledge of the person, or any idea that what I said was right, except that I believed that I was moved by the Spirit to say it; and so striking has been my description, that the persons have gone away, and said to their friends, "Come, see a man that told me all things that I ever did; beyond a doubt, he must have been sent of God to my soul, or else he could not have described me so exactly." And not only so, but I have known many instances in which the thoughts of men have been revealed from the pulpit. I have sometimes seen persons nudge their neighbors with their elbow, because they had got a smart hit, and they have been heard to say, when they were going out, "The preacher told us just what we said to one another when we went in at the door."[1]

Spurgeon was prophesying.

The Old Testament prophet Joel anticipated this unique capacity to know the secrets of another person's heart. He predicted that the gift of prophecy would accompany the outpouring of the Holy Spirit at Pentecost: "I will pour out my Spirit in those days, and they will prophesy."[2] Long after Joel died, the Spirit did come at Pentecost. With his coming also came the ability to prophesy. This should not surprise us: Prophecy is another way the Spirit fulfills Jesus's desire to speak to his community—even about such things as stolen gloves.

Prophecy is one of the special privileges of life in the community of the Spirit. Prophetic words are inspired words that build up and comfort others in the community. They reveal the secrets of a person's heart in a manner that lets the person know God cares about him or her. Because of the power of prophecy, Jesus's followers should eagerly desire the ability to speak into another's life. Prophetic words are given as the conversational community comes together to wait on God and listen to the Spirit. Prophecies can vary greatly in quality, however, and must be tested. By the year AD 100, churches had developed clear criteria for weighing prophecy.[3]

Some people are concerned that prophecy is spiritually risky because it can easily be misinterpreted and even counterfeited. The truth is it *is* risky. Christian author Ken Gire assesses the risk:

> It could be argued…that to open the possibility of God's speaking through other means than the clear teaching of Scripture is to let in all sorts of confusion. After all, a window lets in pollen along with the breeze, flies along with the sunshine, the cackle of crows along with the cooing of doves.

If that were your argument, I would have to agree.

But if we want fresh air, we have to be willing to live with a few flies.

Of course, we can shut out the flies and the pollen and the cackle of crows. And if a clean and quiet house is what's most important to us, perhaps that is what we should do. But if we do, we also shut out so much of the warmth, so much of the fragrance, so many of the sweet songs that may be calling us.[4]

One time at the end of a worship service, I finished speaking and returned to my seat. A picture of a man and a woman came to my mind. I didn't know the woman, but I had met the man. The man and the woman in my vision were looking at each other fondly. I sensed they were not married to each other. Knowing that prophecy must be tested, I decided it wouldn't be wise to speak to these people about this. A mere vision was not reason enough to level such a potentially embarrassing accusation. I concluded that the vision was symbolic of something that might be happening in the church.

I returned to the pulpit and said, "Congregation, please weigh this, for it might be coming from my own mind and not from the Spirit. I'm sensing that there may be a man and a woman here who may be in danger of becoming entangled emotionally."

After the service, a woman approached me with her husband and asked if we could talk. We went to a quiet corner of the room. "I don't know how to say this," she began. "But I think the woman in your vision is me." And then she named the man she felt attracted to.

"Do you mind if I ask you who you saw in your vision?" she asked.

I shuddered. She was the woman I had seen. And the man she named was the man I had seen in the vision.

After the initial confession of her attraction to the other man, she and her husband began to talk honestly about their marriage. Together they decided to find a counselor and work on restoring intimacy to their relationship.

"This is a gift," the couple told me. "God is protecting our marriage." Sounds like Jesus to me.

FEELING GOD'S PLEASURE

The movie *Chariots of Fire* retells the true story of Eric Liddell and Harold Abrahams, two world-class British runners competing for a gold medal at the 1924 Olympic Games in Paris. The film explores how different backgrounds and different faiths influence these two men in their quest for their sport's highest prize.

Liddell's overly religious sister can't grasp her brother's passion for running, so she wants him to reconsider his decision to run in the Olympics and instead return with her to their missionary work in China. Liddell gently replies that he can't give up running, as he says, "When I run I feel his [God's] pleasure."

Deep pleasure is one sign that we are doing what God created us to do. I'm experiencing deep pleasure as I write this book. My wife, Sandi, experiences deep pleasure when she dances. My friend Monroe experiences deep pleasure when he looks at an organizational chart. I met a woman in Vietnam who finds deep pleasure in caring for lepers.

When we discover what gives us deep pleasure we are close to finding what God created us to do. "The voice we should listen to most as we choose a vocation," Frederick Buechner once said in a graduation address, "is the voice of our own gladness. What can we do that makes us the gladdest, what can we do that leaves us with the strongest sense of sailing true north and of peace, which is much of what gladness is? Is it making things with our hands out of wood or stone or paint or canvas?... Or is it making people laugh or weep in a way that cleanses their spirit? I believe that if it is a thing that makes us truly glad, then it is a good thing and it is our thing and it is the calling voice that we were made to answer with our lives."[1]

The New Testament has a name for this passion that rises within us and brings great gladness and pleasure. The biblical phrase is "spiritual gift." Jesus's first act as risen Lord was to pour out the Holy Spirit on his church, and with the Spirit came gifts from the Spirit. "Each one [of us] should use whatever gift he has received to serve others," the apostle Peter wrote in his letter to churches scattered across the Roman Empire, "faithfully administering God's grace in its various forms."[2]

Twenty or so spiritual gifts are mentioned in the letters Paul, Peter, and others wrote in the first century to various churches. Some of these gifts empower members of the community to speak and teach and write about Jesus. Other gifts create an enormous capacity to serve others. Still other spiritual gifts enable some in the community to provide leadership. The lists of specific gifts were not meant to be exhaustive: There are as many different kinds of spiritual gifts as there are people who are empowered by the Holy Spirit.

But remember, these gifts are from the *Spirit;* they are not something we cook up on our own. We scar our souls when we attempt the Spirit's work without the Spirit's gifts. When we succumb to the tyranny of the "oughts" and the "shoulds" and ignore the voice of our own yearning and desire, our service in the community of faith degenerates into joyless slave labor.

But be forewarned: There are plenty of well-meaning people in well-meaning churches who *don't get this.* All manner of manipulative techniques, ranging from guilt to pictures of starving children, are used to get people to buck up and fill a slot because, doggone it, there's a tremendous need and no one else is meeting it! There is a time for taking one for the team, but if you are always taking one for the team, you won't be on the team for long. You'll be bloodied and burned out and frustrated and eager to get as far away from church as you can get.

The gifted writer and educator Parker Palmer describes the early years of his life as a time of "wearing other people's faces." Eager to please others, he became what others wanted him to become but did not live out of his own deep gladness. It took two trips through the dark woods of depression for Palmer to "wear his own face" and pursue a life and ministry that resonated with how God made him. He observes,

> Our deepest calling is to grow into our own authentic selfhood, whether or not it conforms to some image of who we *ought* to be. As we do so, we will not only find the joy that every human seeks—we will also find our path of authentic service in the world.[3]

Life in the community of God's Spirit is made possible by individual lives that are energized by the gifts of the Holy Spirit. The bar is high: We have not become members of the Kiwanis Club. We are to be a community so notable for its radical love and kindness and beauty and hope that the world notices and stops by to ask what's going on. It's not easy to live like that, even on a good day. I am radically kind and loving and hopeful and beautiful when I am on vacation, but I struggle the other fifty weeks of the year.

Jesus knows this. That's why he's given his community spiritual gifts.

BOUNDARIES

Those in my parents' generation know exactly what they were doing when they heard John F. Kennedy had been shot in a Dallas motorcade. Today's generation knows exactly what we were doing when, on the morning of September 11, 2001, al Qaeda terrorists flew three passenger jets into the World Trade Center and the Pentagon and crashed a fourth into a field in Pennsylvania. Everyone agrees the attacks were a defining moment. But what did they define?

The jury is still out regarding the impact September 11 has had on the United States, but one conclusion has found a ready consensus. Radical religion is a dangerous thing. The word *fundamentalism* took on an even more sinister tone in media reports. Americans agree on very little when it comes to religion. But we do agree that we don't like radical fundamentalists who try to do away with everyone who disagrees with them.

A handful of Christian leaders argued in the wake of September 11 that the terrorist attacks prove the inherent moral inferiority of Islam as a religion. These voices subsided when it was quickly, and correctly, pointed out that Christians have also killed "infidels." Like a child who knows there are rogues nested in the branches of his family tree, I've always been ashamed of this part of my spiritual family history. William Manchester, in his marvelous book *A World Lit Only by Fire*, made me sick to my stomach:

Peasants would walk thirty miles to hoot and jeer as a fellow
Christian, enveloped in flames, writhed and screamed his life away.
Afterward the most ardent spectators could be identified by their
own singed hair and features; in their eagerness to enjoy the gamy
scent of burning flesh, they had crowded too close. Ultimately this
fascination with death, as ordinary then as it seems extraordinary
now, led to massive butchery—to spreading bloodstains of religious
wars.... No one has calculated how many sixteenth-century Christians slaughtered other Christians in the name of Christ, but the
gore began to thicken early. [1]

Of course, many people other than Christians have been killed in
religious wars. People of other faiths have been terrorized by the church.
Jews in particular have fallen victim to a series of holocausts and pogroms
because they didn't believe that Jesus is the Messiah. And thousands of
Muslims were slaughtered during the Crusades. In AD 1095, Pope Ur-
ban II called upon Christians to pick up their swords and free the Holy
Land from the infidel. Peter the Hermit spread the message across
Europe, promising eternal life to all who took part. Angry mobs welled
up in cities across Europe, often beginning their long march toward
Jerusalem by slaughtering their Jewish neighbors. Each Crusader wore a
cross as a symbol of his devotion to Jesus. [2]

Although the church has discarded the chain mail in recent centuries, she nevertheless is fighting a covert religious war that is taking
place on two fronts. First, the church is fighting a civil war over issues
ranging from the nature of the bible to whether women should be ordained as elders and clergy. The combatants are typically labeled "conservatives" and "liberals." Churches have split, careers have been destroyed,
and good friends have become enemies over various issues, including the
degree of accuracy in the biblical text and the conflict between evolution
and the creation story in Genesis 1 and 2.

The war's second front is between the church and the world system. This war has been waged in different ways depending on which camp a person is in. Liberal Christians tend to identify the evil world system with racism, sexism, classism, nationalism, and the "military-industrial complex" that builds bombs instead of low-income housing. Conservatives tend to view the enemy as liberalism, secular humanism, moral relativism, feminism, and intellectual elitism.

Thankfully, a new generation of Christians is emerging—a generation that is weary of religious warfare. This generation seeks common ground within the church and respectful relationships outside of it. We are forming churches that emphasize tolerance and respect while holding to orthodox Christian beliefs and practice. Still, the battle doesn't die easily. Even the most tolerant of churches must wrestle with the thorny question of who is in God's kingdom and who isn't. God's kingdom, after all, does not include *everyone*. A community, by definition, has some sort of boundary that marks it off from other communities.

The community of faith that we find in the New Testament recognized such boundaries. "Be wise in the way you act toward outsiders," Paul taught. "Win the respect of outsiders," he said in another place.[3] Jesus spoke of entering the kingdom of heaven and made it clear that some people remain outside of it.[4] What determines who is in and who is out? And can we even have this discussion without heading down the dead-end trail of religious fanaticism and renewed warfare against the infidel?

Twenty years ago Paul Hiebert, a seminary professor who had spent a lifetime wrestling with these questions on the mission field, wrote a groundbreaking essay that answered this question by borrowing from set theory in mathematics.

According to this theory, there are three different types of sets, beginning with the *bounded set*. Bounded sets have clear boundaries. An apple is either an apple or it is not. The main question is whether something is inside or outside the set. Many churches answer the boundary question by establishing bounded sets. They choose a specific list of right beliefs and behaviors that define the members of the community. Everyone who believes and behaves according to the list is inside the community. Those who don't are outside the community.

The second type of set is the *centered set*. Centered sets define a center and the relationship of things to the center. Some things may be far from the center but are moving toward the center and so are part of the centered set. Alternatively, some things may be near the center but are moving away from it; they are not part of the centered set. The set includes only those things that are moving toward the center. In an atom, for example, electrons move toward a positive magnetic pole. They are in the set because they are drawn toward the center.

Churches that solve the boundary question with the centered set approach define their center as Jesus Christ. Who is inside the community? Everyone who is moving toward Jesus Christ. Who is outside the community? Everyone who is moving away from him.

The third type of set is the *fuzzy set*. Fuzzy sets have no sharp boundaries. Things can be half in and half out. For example, a mountain can merge into a plain without evidence of a distinct boundary. Because of the fuzziness of the boundary, a thing can be said to be both on the mountain and on the plain at the same time.

Churches that address the boundary question with the fuzzy-set approach don't draw sharp boundaries. There are no membership lists. You can be both inside and outside the community at the same time. With this view people can be both Christian and Hindu, for instance.

Hiebert says the centered-set approach "seems to correspond most closely with the Hebraic view of reality found in the Bible."[5] The big idea in the bible is not getting the right list but getting the right God and then following him. Jesus did not invite the Galilean fishermen to believe in a doctrine or a list of dogmas. He invited them to believe in him and follow him.

I've been sharing Hiebert's essay with fellow pastors and church leaders. Some of my friends, the ones who are used to living within bounded sets, are concerned about what might happen if we fail to define the boundary with crisp doctrinal and behavioral lists. "Moving toward Jesus" just seems too squishy to them—too ill-defined. Couldn't people fake it? And who's to define what constitutes moving toward Jesus versus moving away from him?

But most of the people I talk to like the idea of the church as a centered set. The church is a faith community on a journey toward Jesus. Everyone who has chosen to walk this journey is in the community, whether they are Catholic or Protestant, Methodist or Episcopalian, Greek Orthodox or participating in an informal house church. It's about the journey of following Jesus. If you're a follower, you're part of the community.

$4,285.78 PER MONTH

Roger and Faith Forster began Icthus Fellowship in a London neighborhood called Council Estates, a depressed area known for violence and drugs. Convinced that the church must minister in both word and deed, the Forsters launched a ministry called Jesus Action. The church posts a Jesus Action phone number all over the neighborhood, offering practical help to anyone who needs it. Church members help with tasks such as gardening, shopping, baby-sitting, and visiting the elderly. They also provide rides to the hospital.

One day a single mother who had just been released from a psychiatric hospital called the Jesus Action number. She needed to launder her clothes and shop for food, and she didn't know how to enroll her six-year-old in school.

"Is this Jesus Action?" she asked Faith over the phone.

"Yes," Faith answered.

"Well," the woman continued, "I want the action, but I don't want the Jesus. I don't want anyone coming here and ramming religion down my throat."

Faith promised that no demands would be placed on the woman. She helped the single mom do her laundry and shop for needed supplies. The woman invited Faith to have tea. Ten minutes later the woman asked, "So what is this about Jesus?" Faith reminded her that they'd agreed not to talk about faith yet. The woman insisted. So Faith told her about her relationship with Jesus.[1] Faith had found the combination of word and deed that are inextricable in the work and proclamation of the church.[2]

After Jesus walked into the synagogue in Nazareth one Sabbath morning, the resident rabbi invited him to speak. He was handed a scroll, which he unrolled until he found these words, penned by the prophet Isaiah:

> The Spirit of the Lord is on me,
>> because he has anointed me
>> to preach good news to the poor.
> He has sent me to proclaim freedom for the prisoners
>> and recovery of sight for the blind,
> to release the oppressed,
>> to proclaim the year of the Lord's favor.

Then Jesus had the audacity to add, "Today this scripture is fulfilled in your hearing."[3]

Jesus modeled a ministry of compassion for hurting people. He brought the good news of the kingdom with both words and actions. "When he saw the crowds," Matthew observed in his gospel, "he had compassion on them, because they were harassed and helpless, like sheep without a shepherd."[4] He fed the hungry and healed the sick. He was concerned with both the bodies and the souls of the people around him.

The early church became known throughout the Roman Empire for its radical acts of kindness toward the needy. The apostle James, writing to the churches a generation after Christ's resurrection, made it clear that the Jesus community is to be marked by its mercy: "Religion that God our Father accepts as pure and faultless is this: to look after orphans and widows in their distress."[5]

It's hard for a twenty-first-century westerner to imagine the chaos and pain of those living in a first-century Greco-Roman city. Ancient cities were remarkably crowded. The population density of Antioch was 117 persons per acre; Rome crammed 200 people into one acre. By contrast, in Chicago today there are 21 residents per acre.[6]

Most city dwellers in the ancient world lived in tiny cubicles in multistoried tenements that lacked fireplaces. Meals were cooked over open fires in the rooms, and since there were no chimneys, the occupants lived in perpetual smoke. Fire was a continual threat, and thousands of people died each year in blazes that spread quickly throughout the tenements.[7]

Sewage systems throughout the Roman Empire consisted of chamber pots that people dumped into the streets at night. Since soap had not yet been invented, sickness was rampant. Life expectancy was less than thirty years, and half of all children died at birth. Nearly every child lost a parent before reaching adulthood. It was very common to see widows and orphans roaming the streets, foraging and begging for food. Death was so prevalent, in fact, that corpses were sometimes abandoned on the streets.[8]

A society that had not yet discovered the existence of germs was highly susceptible to epidemics and plagues. Conservative estimates suggest that a third of the population of the Roman Empire perished in the great plague of AD 165.[9]

The religions of the Roman Empire did not consider mercy one of their core values. The philosopher Seneca thought that drowning children at birth was a reasonable form of controlling the population. Both Plato and Aristotle recommended infanticide as prudent state policy.[10] Mercy was seen as weakness. Christians, however, followed a Messiah who told the first disciples this troubling story:

> When the Son of Man comes in his glory, and all the angels with
> him, he will sit on his throne in heavenly glory. All the nations
> will be gathered before him, and he will separate the people one
> from another as a shepherd separates the sheep from the goats.
> He will put the sheep on his right and the goats on his left.

Then the King will say to those on his right, "Come, you who are blessed by my Father; take your inheritance, the kingdom prepared for you since the creation of the world. For I was hungry and you gave me something to eat, I was thirsty and you gave me something to drink, I was a stranger and you invited me in, I needed clothes and you clothed me, I was sick and you looked after me, I was in prison and you came to visit me."

Then the righteous will answer him, "Lord, when did we see you hungry and feed you, or thirsty and give you something to drink? When did we see you a stranger and invite you in, or needing clothes and clothe you? When did we see you sick or in prison and go to visit you?"

The King will reply, "I tell you the truth, whatever you did for one of the least of these brothers of mine, you did for me."

Then he will say to those on his left, "Depart from me, you who are cursed, into the eternal fire prepared for the devil and his angels. For I was hungry and you gave me nothing to eat, I was thirsty and you gave me nothing to drink, I was a stranger and you did not invite me in, I needed clothes and you did not clothe me, I was sick and in prison and you did not look after me."

They also will answer, "Lord, when did we see you hungry or thirsty or a stranger or needing clothes or sick or in prison, and did not help you?"

He will reply, "I tell you the truth, whatever you did not do for one of the least of these, you did not do for me."

Then they will go away to eternal punishment, but the righteous to eternal life.[11]

Shaped by Christ's compassionate example and haunted by his clear teaching, the early church quickly began to meet the needs of its hurting neighbors. When a plague tore through Alexandria in AD 259, the bishop, Dionysius, described the church's response:

> Most of our brethren did not spare themselves, so great was their brotherly affection. They held fast to each other, visited the sick without fear...and served them for the sake of Christ. Right gladly did they perish with them.... Indeed many did die, after caring for the sick.[12]

The bishop noted that the church's compassionate example was quite a contrast to the way the rest of Rome responded to the plague. "They abandoned those who began to sicken, fled from their dearest friends, threw out the sick when half dead into the streets and let the dead lie unburied."[13]

In his classic 1908 work *The Mission and Expansion of Christianity,* church historian Adolf Harnack carefully recorded ten different ways Christians in the early church cared for the hurting:

- They collected alms and gave them to the poor.
- They supported their own leaders, who then organized charity work.
- They supported widows and orphans.
- They supported the sick, the infirm, the poor, and the disabled.
- They cared for prisoners and those sentenced to the mines.
- They buried the dead when a family could not afford to do so.
- They cared for slaves.
- They cared for people visited by great calamities.
- They provided jobs for the unemployed.
- They cared for brethren on a journey and for churches in poverty or peril.[14]

Israeli-born Ram Cnaan is a professor of social work at the University of Pennsylvania. Cnaan, who makes it clear that he is not committed to any religion, became interested in the role American churches play in caring for the poor and needy. He visited congregations and interviewed them about their ministry to their neighbors. Nearly every congregation he surveyed was involved in providing mercy ministries to the surrounding community. The most common programs addressed the needs of children, the elderly, the poor, and the homeless. Cnaan suggests that were it not for the work of churches, approximately one-third of children now in day-care centers would have no place to go, many Twelve Step groups would lose their meeting places, and large numbers of soup kitchens and homeless shelters would disappear. He goes so far as to put a price tag on the various services the average church in America gives freely to its community: $4,285.78 per month.[15]

Other studies are beginning to tell an often-overlooked story: Churches really do serve their communities. One found that 75 percent of the members of churches interviewed had participated in "social service, community development or neighborhood organizing projects" within the past twelve months.[16] Another study reported that "nearly 85 percent of all U.S. congregations are engaged with soup kitchens or food pantries, emergency shelters and clothing pantries, and with financial help to those in need."[17]

These findings would not surprise the members of Concord Baptist Church, a congregation that helps meet the needs of the Bedford-Stuyvesant section of Brooklyn. "People are involved in our church because our church is involved in community development," says pastor Gary Simpson.[18]

Concord Baptist was born in a living room in 1847 when a small group of Christians came together to see how they could serve their neighborhood. Enslaved African Americans who fled north found a safe haven at Concord Baptist long before the Emancipation Proclamation. Realizing that illiteracy was a major problem, Concord members established a school to teach anyone who wanted to learn how to read. In 1877

Concord Baptist created the Dorcas Home Missionary Society to provide food, clothing, and money to those who needed it. When juvenile delinquency became a problem in the 1930s, Concord responded with scouting programs, vacation bible school, and sports camps for youth.

Beginning in the mid-1900s, Concord members developed nine not-for-profit corporations to meet specific needs in their community. Many times these programs came about in response to the pain of racism. In 1951, for example, a small group of Concord members came together to share their hurt and anger at being turned down for loans. The eight-member group began a credit union with forty dollars in share deposits. Today, the Concord Federal Credit Union has almost one thousand members and assets of close to three million dollars.

What has motivated the people of Concord Baptist to give a century and a half of compassionate service to their corner of Brooklyn? "We are challenged by Jesus to let our light so shine that others may see our good works and glorify our Father in heaven," explains pastor Gary Simpson. "We are a social outreach church, so ministry opportunities are themselves worship stations."[19]

The community that is made up of Jesus's followers has a two-thousand-year tradition of caring for the needs of its neighbors. Dr. Ram Cnaan was asked what surprised him most about his research. Among the surprises, he noted, was the inaccuracy of one of his own assumptions. "I was expecting them [churches] to be providing social services primarily in order to persuade people to change their religion and become members. This assumption was simply wrong."[20]

Perhaps the time has arrived for the church to become known not as a special-interest group clamoring for its rights but as a caring community meeting the needs of its neighbors.

CAMUS FINDS THE EXIT

J ean-Paul Sartre's play *No Exit* opens with Mr. Garcin being escorted to his room by the valet. Within a few lines of dialogue, we discover that Garcin actually has been escorted into hell. Before long, he is joined by Inez, a crusty post-office clerk, and Estelle, an insecure socialite who can't exist without a mirror to use for checking her makeup. It soon dawns on the three guests that they are going to spend eternity together in this room.

As the room grows warmer, Garcin suggests they share their stories to explain what they did to deserve the sentence of hell. Perhaps this will help them get along better. Garcin deserted from the war and died poorly before a firing squad. Estelle drowned an unwanted baby. Inez had an affair with a married man. The characters fake authentic caring and quickly begin fighting. Hell isn't at all what they expected. Garcin figures out the pathetic joke first. "So this is hell. I'd never have believed it. You remember all we were told about the torture-chambers, the fire and brimstone, the 'burning marl.' Old wives' tales! There's no need for red-hot pokers. Hell is—other people!"[1]

All communities have a tendency to turn inward and destroy themselves. This is equally true of the church. The church exists for the world, and when she forgets that, the room warms up, shared confessions become weapons of betrayal, and love turns to manipulation.

"The first act of the risen Lord was to breathe the Spirit on the disciples and send them forth into mission," theologian Clark Pinnock reminds us. "God did not pour the Spirit out for our private benefit.... The church exists...for the world."[2]

As Jesus told his disciples shortly before he ascended into heaven, "You will receive power when the Holy Spirit comes on you; and you will be my witnesses in Jerusalem, and in all Judea and Samaria, and to the ends of the earth."[3]

That is exactly what happened. The people who had been with Jesus began to tell their friends about him. This came about naturally, through conversation as they forged a horseshoe or drew water from a well. A generation later, communities of Christ's disciples had sprung up across the Roman Empire as one friend told another friend about Jesus.

When I was little my parents tried to tell me about Jesus. They would get me up early on Sunday morning, put me in my best corduroys and Buster Browns and take me to the Methodist Church on High Street, just up the block from the Worthington Bakery. I was in church, but I wasn't ready to listen.

Fifteen years later, in the spring of 1976, Worthington High School was selling expensive chocolate bars as a fund-raiser. Doug Martin had a free coupon for a Burger King Whopper that he'd gotten from the wrapper of one of those chocolate bars, and he invited me to lunch. Over burgers Doug told me about Jesus. He invited me to attend "Fifth Quarter," his church youth group that met on Friday nights. I think it got its name because it began meeting after the football games in the fall. It had a reputation for attracting good-looking sophomore girls from Grace Brethren Church's Christian school. So, wooed with a Whopper and anxious to connect with pretty girls, I showed up at Mr. Widow's house that Friday night. And on a Friday night, as Mr. Widow prayed in his living room, I became a follower of Jesus Christ.

That's how it happens, usually. Parents tell their children, friends tell their friends, and people get to know Jesus. New communities spring up. The gospel spreads.

But it's not always that easy. Jesus tells the church to be his witnesses "to the ends of the earth." We have not fulfilled our mission when we have told our friends. Jesus asks us to talk about him in cultures that have never heard of him.

Patrick was a carefree sixteen-year-old living on the coast of Britain early in the fifth century when pirates captured him and sold him into slavery in Ireland. He escaped seven years later and fled to a monastery in France. One evening Patrick had a dream. A letter appeared and was read by Irish voices. The voices begged, "We beseech thee holy youth, to come and walk with us once more." Patrick returned to the land of his captivity and spent the rest of his life traveling from village to village telling people about Jesus. We remember Patrick every March 17 on Saint Patrick's Day.

Fulfilling Christ's mission to tell people around the world about him has been costly. Missionaries to malaria-ridden Africa in the late nineteenth century packed their belongings in a coffin because odds were they'd be needing one. Members of the eighteenth century Moravian community sold themselves into slavery to tell slaves in the West Indies about Jesus. And I am reminded of Katie Couric's interview with a missionary who had watched her colleagues being beheaded by guerrilla captors in the Philippines.

The mission is costly. Yet the mission is worth it, because people are worth it.

The French writer Albert Camus was as well known as Sartre for his brilliant existentialist writings. Camus wrote three major novels—*The Stranger* (1942), *The Plague* (1947), and *The Fall* (1956)—before his tragic death in a car accident in 1960. His novels painted a chilling picture of a stark, meaningless world.

In the final year of his life, the great writer sought out Howard

Mumma, the guest minister at the American Church in Paris, for spiritual discussion. Camus discussed how hard it was for him to believe in God when there was so much suffering in the world. Mumma shared that he, too, was troubled by suffering and had no easy answer for Camus' questions. At a later visit, Camus said to Mumma, "I am searching for something I do not have, something I'm not sure I can identify." Then he asked, "What does 'you must be born again' mean?"

Mumma replied that it meant "to enter afresh into the process of spiritual growth…to receive forgiveness because you have asked God to forgive you for your sins."

"Howard," the great writer replied, "I'm ready. I want this."[4]

Albert Camus had found the exit.

THE SACRAMENT
OF BELONGING

Howard, do you perform baptisms?" Albert Camus asked Reverend Howard Mumma. The famous existentialist wanted to know more: What did baptism mean? Could he be baptized secretly?

Mumma was torn. Camus had mentioned that he had already been baptized before he had left the Christian faith. One baptism, Mumma thought, was enough. Besides, the Methodist minister didn't like the idea of a secret baptism.

"Baptism is a symbolic commitment to God," he explained. As a mark of commitment, it is necessarily a *public* decision that a person is entering a community of faith. He asked Camus for a little more time for both of them to pursue these questions and come to a common mind. Camus drove Mumma to the airport, promising to pick up the discussion the following year when Mumma returned to Paris. "I am going to keep striving for the Faith," Camus told Mumma as the minister boarded the plane for Ohio.[1]

It was their last meeting. A few months later, on January 4, 1960, Camus died in an auto accident.

"Repent and be baptized, every one of you, in the name of Jesus Christ for the forgiveness of your sins," the apostle Peter told the thousands who converted to Christianity in response to the church's first sermon. "And you will receive the gift of the Holy Spirit."[2]

Albert Camus rightly identified baptism as the initiation rite into the Christian church. Some readers of his 1956 novel, *The Fall*, wondered if the renowned atheist was beginning to turn toward Christianity. If so, he never explicitly spoke of his spiritual journey in print. Camus first went to Mumma's church in the early 1950s to hear the famous organist Marcel Dupré. Pleasantly surprised and intrigued by Mumma's preaching, the Nobel Prize winner asked for a lunch date, and a remarkable friendship was born. Camus began to read the bible for the first time in his life. The two men continued meeting to discuss what it said. Mumma remained silent about their talks for forty years.

Camus revealed his struggles with Christianity in his famous novel *The Plague*. Oran, a French port city on the Algerian coast, is overcome with the plague. The priest of Oran, Father Paneloux, tells his flock to submit to the disease as God's punishment. "And while a good many adapted themselves to confinement and carried on their humdrum lives as before, there were others who rebelled and whose one idea now was to break loose from the prison house."[3]

Camus couldn't believe a good and loving God would allow suffering. So he concluded that God didn't exist and that life is ultimately meaningless. We can create meaning, however, by doing something ourselves about the suffering around us. We can fight the plague, even if the church remains passive, mumbling incoherent phrases about it being "the will of God."

Perhaps Camus' conversations with Howard Mumma helped him see that the church he'd rejected in *The Plague* was a caricature of the real thing and that the real church he was moving toward could be an ally in the war against the plague of human suffering.

"In a word, our very existence seems absurd," he confessed to Mumma.[4] Perhaps he saw in the church a community of meaning in an absurd world and longed to be a member of it. We'll never know. We do know that he rightly identified baptism as the initiation rite into the community of Christ. It has been this way from the start.[5]

A first-century document known as the Didache, passed among early church leaders as a kind of primer for new churches, gave precise directions to "baptize in the name of the Father and of the Son and of the Holy Spirit."[6] Baptism was—and is—the sign and symbol that the new believer had been joined to the new community.

Perhaps Camus, who wrote so powerfully about the alienation of modern life in *The Stranger,* simply was tired of being alone. Baptism is an invitation to strangers everywhere to return home. It welcomes us into a community in which we do not live or die alone.

Yet baptism is more than a celebration of homecoming. It is also a celebration of forgiveness. The community that baptism initiates us into is the community of the forgiven, a community of people who have been washed clean from the stain of their sins.

Camus' last major novel, *The Fall,* is an exploration of human sin. The story takes place in a seedy Amsterdam bar where a Paris lawyer, Jean-Baptiste Clamence, delivers a stark monologue to an unknown listener. The longer he talks, the more Clamence reveals. Outwardly respectable, Clamence describes himself as a hypocrite.

There is no happy ending. Clamence, exposed, has no cure for his dark heart.

Camus wrote *The Fall* during the years he was secretly exploring the spiritual health of his own heart with Howard Mumma. Perhaps the Amsterdam bar became a confessional where he probed the depths of his own sin through the musings of Clamence. We will never know.

He apparently could not live in the moral empty place in which Clamence is left at the end of *The Fall.* Like his fictional lawyer, Camus knew his own heart was fallen as well. He sought forgiveness.

Hence the startling question from one of the great atheists of the twentieth century: "Howard, do you perform baptisms?"

WEEPING WILLOWS

Nike pays Tiger Woods millions of dollars a year to wear the Swoosh, because Nike knows the power of symbols. Symbols are much more powerful than signs. Signs just stand for something else, like solving for x in an algebraic equation.

In contrast, symbols are alive. They communicate. They connect. They touch us in ways signs never do. Nike grasps the psychology of symbols: Somehow, middle-aged insurance adjusters who've never broken one hundred on a golf course will buy Nike clubs because the symbol gives them an emotional connection with Tiger. Symbols have a way of elevating us, if only in our imaginations.

Symbols can evoke feelings of pride and patriotism. I choke back tears every time I see the image of the three New York City firefighters raising the American flag amidst the smoldering rubble of the World Trade Center. Symbols can also terrify us. A burning cross in the yard of a black family is a horrific abuse of the power of symbols. A swastika spray-painted on a Jewish synagogue conjures up the demons of the Holocaust for everyone who has ever worn the Star of David.

Symbols help us experience God, too. "Human beings are symbol users, and God is a symbol maker," observes Clark Pinnock.[1] The Lord's Supper is a powerful symbol through which we, the symbol users, encounter God, a symbol maker.

The Lord Jesus, on the night he was betrayed, took bread, and when he had given thanks, he broke it and said, "This is my body, which is for you; do this in remembrance of me." In the same way, after supper he took the cup, saying, "This cup is the new covenant in my blood; do this, whenever you drink it, in remembrance of me." For whenever you eat this bread and drink this cup, you proclaim the Lord's death until he comes.[2]

When we participate in the Lord's Supper, we remember Jesus's death on our behalf. But it is a different kind of remembering. It's not high-school field-trip remembering, where you visit a battle site from the Revolutionary War and are reminded to be thankful for the sacrifice the soldiers made for our freedom. (*I really ought to be more thankful for that,* we say to ourselves. *I wonder what's for lunch?*)

The remembering we do in the Lord's Supper is more like the remembering lovers do when they recall their first kiss, or the remembering parents do when they come across a broken, forgotten toy and time collapses and for a moment their teenager is a toddler again.

Lord's Supper remembering is the remembering of mystery. Something mysterious happens when we take the Lord's Supper with faith that the Spirit of God brings Jesus to us in the bread and cup. "I am the bread of life," Jesus said. "He who comes to me will never go hungry."[3] We feed on the Bread of Life when we come to the communion table. We are nourished. We find healing. We are prepared to go out into the world again.

The symbol of the Lord's Supper is rather tame if you only approach it from the earthly side of the mystery. It's a nice way to remember something God did for you long ago. Sort of like recalling the heroics of George Washington when you visit Valley Forge. The Lord's Supper is transformed into a life-giving power, though, when you encounter it on the other side of mystery. Jesus meets us in the bread and the cup, meets us again, and meets us afresh, meets us to feed us and to prepare us for works of mercy and witness. He meets us in a way he doesn't meet us when we don't take communion, or when we take it without an appreciation for the mystery of God's work.

Yet what is it that really happens when we take the bread and the cup by faith, trusting in the Spirit to connect us with Christ? No one really knows. Christ is there, as Martin Luther put it, under the bread and the wine. To ask how he is there is to ask too much. He is there. That is enough.

Hear how Justin Marytr described the mystery in AD 150:

> For not as common bread and common drink do we receive
> these; but in like manner as Christ our Savior, having been made
> flesh by the Word of God, was made both flesh and blood for our
> salvation, so likewise have we been taught that the food which is
> blessed by the prayer of His word, and from which our blood and
> flesh by transformation are nourished, is the flesh and blood of
> that Jesus who was made flesh.[4]

How does this happen? I don't know. It's a mystery.

My mother-in-law, Barb, was struck down with a strange disease of the mind. Norm, her husband, heroically cared for his bride for seven years until Barb's physicians drew the line. Today Barb lies quietly in an Alzheimer's facility just off the main street of Foley, Alabama, shaded, not ironically, by weeping willows. Barb has not been able to attend her church for many months. Her eighty-year-old pastor, however, didn't forget her. In the days when Barb was still alert enough to interact with visitors, her pastor would park his car beneath one of the willows, walk through the entrance doors with the sign that says, "The season is summer. The year is 2001," past the lounge where someone's parents sit slumped in their wheelchairs as a TV game-show host invites contestants to "come on down." He'd turn right at the nurses' station crowded with rows of blue pill cups and enter Barb's room, bearing the gifts of the bread and the cup.

"This is my body, which is for you."

"This cup is the new covenant in my blood; do this, whenever you drink it, in remembrance of me."

SAVING TIME

I didn't think about time much until I turned forty. Now I think about time all the time. I think about how quickly time drains through the hourglass. I think about how much sand has already slipped away. I think about how I can't tell how much sand is left. Each day brings fresh reminders of sand slipping away.

The bottom right-hand drawer beneath my bathroom sink, the drawer underneath the drawer where I keep my toothpaste, razors, and over-the-counter pain reliever, is a drawer filled with miniature plastic animals. There are lions and zebras in that drawer. Even an elephant, a chimpanzee, and a gorilla. I think a bunny's down there, and probably a duck. Lest you think it strange for a middle-aged man to have toy animals in the drawer beneath his sink, let me explain. In years past my children hated taking baths. So we bought them plastic animals and dumped them in the tub. Dirty knees became mountain peaks towering above the white snows of bubble bath, from which unsuspecting mountain lions plunged to watery deaths. Cheeks and noses poked up from the froth, islands in a bubbly sea. An occasional volcano of soapy water would spew from the deep by the hot breath of a submerged three-year-old, soaking the gods presiding over this watery universe.

I opened the bottom-right drawer awhile ago to look for a fingernail clipper and stumbled headlong into the plastic zoo that once made bathtime bearable in our house. This evoked a memory of what we once did that we do no more. Time is not just hands moving on a clock. Time has meaning.

"By itself," writes Alexander Schmemann, "time is nothing but a line of telegraph poles strung out into the distance and at some point along the way is our death."[1]

In the church, time is not regarded in isolation as if it has no higher value or spiritual purpose. The church redeems time, makes it holy, gives it hope, by building into the seemingly meaningless line of telegraph poles reminders that God has entered into time to save it and give it meaning. The early church began to redeem time by setting aside Sunday, the first day of the week, for worship. Judaism, the cradle of Christianity, had worshiped God on the Sabbath Saturday because God himself had rested on the seventh day of creation. Christians moved their day of rest and worship to Sunday because it was the day Jesus rose from the dead.

In October 1992 I had the opportunity to spend a week with pastor Raylu Gacea in Tulcea, Romania, a forgotten industrial city rusting to death on the southern shore of the Black Sea. Hobbled women in black coats and scarves waited for hours in bread lines. Silent, sad, dark-eyed men smoked unfiltered cigarettes in cafés with no lights. Low, angry clouds the color of dying fish cloaked the city with an oppressive canopy. No one smiled. No one laughed. No one looked you in the eye. Romania in the fall of 1992 had not yet begun to awaken from its seventy-year nightmare with Communism.

One evening as we drank hot tea at his kitchen table, Raylu talked about what it was like to be a Christian in Romania under Nicolae Ceauçescu's dictatorship. Raylu spoke of the fear of being taken away at night, of spies in his congregation, of friends he'd never see again, of his concerns for his children. And then, almost in passing, he remembered a quieter horror: Ceauçescu had banned Sundays as a day of rest and worship, demanding that the nation work seven days a week to meet the quotas of the government planners. The dictator had killed time. Life became an unending blur of telegraph poles. A heavy psychic depression settled on the good people of Romania.

We need Sunday, or at least some day of the week, that we set aside for rest, worship, family, and friends. The rhythm of Sunday gives us a sense of endings and beginnings, of completion and fresh starts. Weekly worship reminds us that even though the sands are slipping through the glass, the end of time is not death but life, or at the very least physical death that leads to life beyond death.

My friends surprised me on my fortieth birthday with a barbeque and a roast—of me. My prankster friends Jim and Toni took a video camera into Borders bookstore and asked an army of sales clerks to help them find one of the books I had authored, which, of course, was nowhere to be found. Then came the gifts: neatly wrapped packages of Depend adult diapers, Grecian Formula for my rapidly graying hair, Ex-Lax for, well, you get the idea. My friends love me, even if they don't read my books, and I was thankful for the evening.

Birthdays are one way we mark time, but they don't save time or fill it with joy. Left to themselves, birthdays are nothing more than a way to count the telegraph poles you're passing on the way to the horizon of death.

The church year marks time in a different way, noting not just one individual's march through time but recalling the God who came into time to save it. Three great holidays have traditionally marked the Christian church's calendar: Christmas, celebrating the birth of Christ; Easter, celebrating the death and resurrection of Christ; and Pentecost, celebrating the gift of the Holy Spirit to the church. These days were called feast days in the early church, and they were days of great joy. Alexander Schmemann writes, "For the man of the past a feast was not something...additional: it was his way of putting meaning into his life, of liberating it from the animal rhythm of work and rest."[2]

The further I push past forty, the more I am drawn to the deep and ancient rhythms of the Christian calendar. (I sometimes slip away to the liturgical churches in town to satisfy this primal need. There is a renewing and healing rhythm to the cadence of the ancient liturgy of worship.) The sacred ebb and flow of the Christian year, rooted in Christ's coming, dying, rising, and giving of the Spirit reminds me of a time above this time, a time that is hopeful and triumphant regardless of whether I wind up wearing adult diapers.

So important was the sacred use of time to the early Christians that they ordered each day around a rhythm of remembrance, worship, Scripture reading, and prayer. This ordering of the day around prayer was called the Divine Office or the Liturgy of the Hours and was mostly practiced in monasteries, each prayer time having a Latin name. The day began with Vigils before dawn and then was followed by Lauds. After breakfast prayer was held at nine (Terce), noon (Sext), and three (None). Vespers was sung in the evening. The community ended the day with Compline at night.

Today it is all but impossible to order our days around these ancient patterns of prayer. Yet many believers are drawing from these ancient traditions in an attempt to bring order to their hectic days and nights. I've begun praying morning, noon, and evening using the *Book of Common Prayer* as a guide. Living within these ancient rhythms does indeed have a way of making the day more holy.

I will always feel a kind of grief when I encounter a plastic mountain lion in my bathroom drawer. But it is a gentle grief, made kinder and more hopeful by a God who has entered time to save it.

HOPE

Kurt Cobain had given up hope. The twenty-seven-year-old founder of the rock group Nirvana had grown weary of a world he found cruel and unfair, fans who didn't understand him, and a drug addiction he couldn't kick. He bought a shotgun at a Seattle sporting-goods store, took some drugs for the last time, and ended his life. He left the following note:

> Thank you all from the pit of my burning, nauseous stomach for your letters and concern during the past years.... I don't have the passion anymore. So remember, it's better to burn out than rust out.... I'm so sorry. Please don't follow me.
>
> Peace, love, empathy,
>
> Kurt Cobain[1]

The doctor who examined Cobain's body noted that this was "the act of someone wanting to obliterate himself, to literally become nothing."[2]

Cobain journaled prolifically in spiral notebooks about his music, his relationships, his addictions, and his struggle with despair. The journals remained locked in a safe until 2002, when Riverhead Books published them. The journal entries paint a portrait of a brilliant, tormented young man increasingly losing a battle with hopelessness. Here are some of the entries:

> And this little pit-stop we call life that we so seriously worry about is nothing but a small, over the weekend jail sentence compared to what will come with death.

> Man is not redeemable.

> I wish there was somebody I could ask advice, someone who wouldn't make me feel like a creep for spilling my guts and trying to explain the insecurities that have plagued me for oh, about 25 years now. I wish somebody could explain to me why I used to have so much energy.

> I hate myself and want to die. Leave me alone.[3]

Cobain's dark pessimism fueled his songwriting and gave birth to the grunge rock movement. His words and music reflect the way a lot of people feel about life on Planet Earth: hopeless.

There are somber reasons for the erosion of hope. Terrorists pledge to spill more blood on American soil. Meanwhile, AIDS ravages southern Africa in what Senator Bill Frist has called "a plague of biblical proportions. And it has only begun to wreak its destruction upon humanity."[4] North Korea sends mixed signals about its nuclear program, and the rest of the world feels a shiver. The global population is soaring: Africa is projected to be the fastest-growing continent by 2110, yet food production actually decreased in Africa in the 1980s. Famines have ravished Ethiopia and Somalia. Forests are disappearing and becoming desert. Terms such as *acid rain, toxic waste,* and *greenhouse gases* are now part of our everyday vocabulary, and everyone knows something is wrong with the ozone layer, though most of us don't know what.

Life is hard at home, too. Wonderful couples who have loved each other for years find themselves in divorce court, arguing over the kids. The economy sputters, and good people lose good jobs. Aging parents are diagnosed with debilitating illnesses. A routine checkup reveals a tumor in the lung of a friend's eight-year-old daughter.

It's not hard to understand why millions of Americans take antidepressants. This is a depressing world. Is there any hope?

Hope is one of many gifts the Jews have given to the world. The neighbors of ancient Israel lacked hope. They believed life followed a rhythmic cycle of repeated, inescapable events. The Canaanites, for example, primarily worshiped two gods, whose activities were linked to seasons of the year. During the early summer, when desert air began to dry out the crops, the Canaanites mourned the death of the fertility god Baal and observed the triumph of Mot, the god of death. When winter rains returned and once again brought the promise of good crops, the birth of Baal was celebrated. Then they started all over again.

God taught Israel to view life differently. Life was not an endless repetition of the same repeatable seasons. Rather, God had broken into history, and history was going somewhere. Despite the disappointments and uncertainties of life, there was a discernible plot unfolding from creation to the end of time. History was no longer random or meaningless. God was telling a story through history.

Today, because we know we are part of this Great Story that ultimately ends in a good place, we have hope. But Kurt Cobain would have disagreed. And he would not have been alone.

Could the Jews be wrong? Sigmund Freud thought they were. The founder of psychoanalysis believed we fabricate the whole God-thing because we need to. The God of hope, he argued, was mere human wish

fulfillment. We want there to be a God who is working in the
we invent him.

Was Freud right? Do we have any reason for hope?

The early Christians placed their hope in Jesus Christ. His miraculous and sinless life, his sacrificial death on the cross, his resurrection from
the dead, and his ascension into heaven convinced them that their Lord
was no mere man but was in fact the Son of God breaking into history.
Paul believed the resurrection is the reason for our hope.

> And if Christ has not been raised, our preaching is useless and so
> is your faith.... And if Christ has not been raised, your faith is
> futile; you are still in your sins.... If only for this life we have
> hope in Christ, we are to be pitied more than all men.
>
> But Christ has indeed been raised from the dead, the first-
> fruits of those who have fallen asleep. For since death came
> through a man, the resurrection of the dead comes also through a
> man. For as in Adam all die, so in Christ all will be made alive.
> But each in his own turn: Christ, the firstfruits; then, when he
> comes, those who belong to him. Then the end will come, when
> he hands over the kingdom to God the Father after he has
> destroyed all dominion, authority and power. For he must reign
> until he has put all his enemies under his feet. The last enemy to
> be destroyed is death.[5]

The resurrection is the heart of Christian hope because it validates
that the Author of history is still alive and busy writing the ending. The
resurrection declares that God is loose, alive, and free. He is still active
in the chaotic life of our planet. The church, then, is to be a community
of hope.

Ben came to our Bible-study group trying to conceal his emotions, but he couldn't keep his game face on for long. He'd had a terrible week. Had anything good happened? the rest of us wanted to know.

"Yes," Ben said. He'd been to a funeral the day before.

Nervous laughter filled the awkward silence; we waited for the punch line. There was no punch line, but there was a story of hope that moved us all.

Jennifer, a vivacious forty-year-old mother of triplets, had yielded to the cancer that had been threatening her life for a year. But she never did yield her soul to the disease.

Ben described what happened in Jennifer's life during her final, pain-wracked year. She had rediscovered God, met him in ways she'd never dreamed possible as she wandered the dark side of the moon. Jennifer knew she was dying when she visited Disney World for a final family vacation. She knew she was dying at Christmas. She knew she was dying when she saw the dogwoods bloom for the last time.

Yet Jennifer had found hope. She became more deeply involved in a church whose good people nurtured her hope, even as her medical hopes grew dim. Jennifer's hope grew until it began to spill onto others who seemed more terrified of her dying than she was. Ben could barely control his emotions as he described how Jennifer opened her living room to the young mothers she did life with. Sacred things happen in a dying woman's house. You ask the questions you don't ask in Sunday school. You pray in ways you don't usually pray. Together, Jennifer and her friends walked toward God. They walked toward death. And in their walking they found hope.

The funeral, Ben concluded, had been a celebration of Jennifer's life and the friends and family she shared it with. And Jennifer's story gave him hope during a dark time in his own life.

Jennifer died in a community that nurtured her hope.

Kurt Cobain died alone. But it didn't have to be that way.

WHAT I LEARNED FROM SEAN

I was leading a bible class, and one morning they asked me, "Can you teach us about Islam?"

"Sure," I said. I was lying.

I didn't know much about Islam. I'd never read the Koran. I'd never been to a Muslim prayer service. Panicking, I e-mailed a professor friend in the University of Tennessee religious studies department. "Rosalind," I pleaded, "do you have anyone in your department in Islamic studies who might give me a crash course on what Muslims believe?"

"Yes," she e-mailed back. "Sean Blevins."

Sean and I arranged to have lunch at the Sunspot (where tie-dyes and neckties hang out, the radio spot says). I wasn't sure what an Islamic studies professor living in eastern Tennessee would look like. I arrived early and took a seat facing the door. A few minutes after noon, a man in his late twenties entered. He had a neatly trimmed beard and moustache and was wearing a dark navy traditional Muslim jacket and hat. He looked like a visiting graduate student from the Middle East, though with lighter complexion.

"Sorry I'm late," he said softly, blue eyes smiling behind frameless glasses. "I've just finished teaching my class. I'm honored that you want to talk."

Sean ordered coffee, noting that he normally doesn't eat lunch, while I ordered "Today's Soup Made Fresh Yesterday" and a Caesar salad.

We discussed the class I was teaching, what their questions were, and the stereotypes we struggled with since September 11 and the Iraq War. We shared our common passions for unity within the city. I shared my desire to do doctoral work on new models of partnership within the Christian faith community; he replied that he was interested in PhD studies of how Muslims, Jews, and Christians worked and lived together in peace in Spain during the Middle Ages. His answers were measured and thoughtful, usually followed up with a question about what I believed. Here was a face to Islam that I didn't see in most of the news footage shown on CNN.

By the time I finished my soup, I knew two things:

Sean Blevins is a very special man.

I can learn from him.

I had arrogantly assumed that I could interview Sean, ask him for a book or two, and then teach an introduction to his religion. I'm embarrassed to admit my hubris; I wouldn't want someone who didn't know anything about Christianity to teach it to their friends after having lunch with me and reading a book or two. You can never truly understand someone else's religion unless it is explained to you by *a believer*.

I asked Sean to come in and teach for me. He handed me a book titled *The Way of Islam,* written, he explained, by a scholar from Iran who'd studied at Cambridge and wanted to explain Islam to Western minds. Perhaps our group could go through this book first and then meet with Sean for several sessions. Helping others understand his faith was important to him.

"Sean," I asked as the waiter took the check, "can I ask you a personal question?"

He smiled. "Yes. Go on."

"Can you tell me how you converted to Islam?"

Sean told me he had been interested in the spiritual life from a young age, even reading Huston Smith's *Religions of the World* while still in junior high school. The traditional, southern, conservative churches in his East Tennessee town never appealed to him. Arriving at the University of Tennessee, he devoured the religion classes, especially enjoying studies on the early church. He converted to Catholicism and began reading extensively in Catholic theology and philosophy. He enjoyed the Catholic Church's intellectual rigor, he said, and its openness to transcendence and mystery.

Several years passed. Sean read even more deeply into the doctrinal discussions of the church's first centuries, especially the debates about the trinity.

"The trinity never made sense to me," Sean told me. No matter how much he read, he couldn't get over an intellectual stumbling block: How could God be both three and one?

Sean was exposed to Islam in a class on world religions. He was drawn to its simplicity, he said, its holistic view of life. Muslims worship one God. Allah is his name. The five pillars of Islam, five key spiritual disciplines ranging from fasting to serving the poor, marked the path of obedience. Perhaps most important, Islam does not demand belief in the trinity. In Islam, God is one being.

"That made more sense to me," Sean said. "A lot more sense." And so Sean became a Muslim. He lives a few blocks from our city's only mosque, sharing a one-bedroom apartment with a fellow Muslim graduate student. The living room is vacant except for a prayer rug, where you'll find him five times a day, bowing toward Mecca.

Our class with Sean turned out to be a great success. With bibles and Koran open, we learned about our faith as we learned about his. One of the members of the group, Hallerin, hosts a popular radio talk show. During the weeks we were studying Islam with Sean, an angry caller phoned Hallerin and began trashing the Muslims in our community.

"That's not true," Hallerin told the caller. "I've just been studying Islam with one of their leaders. You don't understand what they believe or how they live."

I now consider Sean Blevins a friend. I want to have lunch again with him soon. By teaching me his faith, he helped me understand better what I believe about my own.

Sean is not the first person to be turned off by the tedious, speculative, combative arguments about the nature of the trinity that seem to be locked in the language and thought patterns of another time. Perhaps our forefathers tried to explain too much; perhaps they tried to explain the unexplainable. The trinity, Sean's stumbling block with Christianity, is for me God's most beautiful dimension. God is love. To be love God must love. But who does God love? People? Yes, to be sure, but God existed long before he created people. God is love because God is a community in which the Father, Son, and Spirit all love one another. The three members of the trinity exist in loving society with one another.

We find the first outline of the trinity in the first three verses of the book of Genesis. In Genesis 1:1 we are introduced to God, the designer of all creation. The second verse describes "the Spirit of God" hovering over the earth. In verse 3 we meet yet another dimension of God: the Word of God. God speaks, and the world comes into existence. The rest of the bible, especially the New Testament, adds texture and detail to the portrait of these three Persons as they live together as the One God of Israel.

The early church wrestled to bring together three strands of belief. First, there was monotheism, the belief that God is one. Then there was their belief that Jesus was himself God and Lord. And third was their experience of the Holy Spirit as the Spirit of God. The doctrine of the trinity was the result.

For me it boils down to this: God exists in a loving, self-giving community. Therefore, we should too. We, who are God's image bearers, must live in community with one another. "I pray...that all of them may be one, Father, just as you are in me and I am in you," Jesus prayed, "...so that the world may believe that you have sent me."[1]

When we love one another like the members of the trinity love one another, the world catches a glimpse of God. "Because he is community he creates community," writes theologian Gilbert Bilezikian. "Therefore, the making of community may not be regarded as an optional decision for Christians."[2] The life of God is expressed in the community we call the church.

I do not reveal the God of love to the world when I sit in my study reading books about God or listening to tapes of sermons that attempt to describe God. I reveal the God of love when I love; and love demands that I be a member of the community of faith, the church. I will always be a part of a faith community because it is in that community that I am most in touch with the nature of God.

Some of the early church's efforts to explain the trinity are helpful as we try to unpack what it means to live in community as God is community. John of Damascus, writing in the eighth century, used the word *perichoresis* to describe the loving way the members of the trinity relate to one another. The word means "interdependent" or "interpenetration." The three members of the Godhead are interdependent. They are partners; they are mutually dependent on one another; they live as one with each other in intimate ways while always retaining their identities as separate Persons. They interpenetrate one another.

This is the church's model for loving well as a community. We come together as diverse people: liberal and conservative, wealthy and poor, Hummer drivers and Harley riders. We become one within our diversity by being mutually dependent on one another, by sharing our lives in intimate ways, by partnering, while at the same time remaining distinct persons.

The early church also thought long and hard about roles within the trinity. The question, specifically, was this: Is the trinity a hierarchy, with the Son submitting to the Father for all eternity? Or is the trinity a mutually interdependent partnership, with each member mutually submitting to one another? Three theologians, Gregory the Great, Gregory of Nazianzus, and Basil the Great, from a city in what is now Turkey, helped answer this question in the fourth century. The church agreed that while Christ submitted himself for a season to the Father for the purpose of his work on earth, this was not eternal submission. There is no hierarchy in the trinity; there is partnership, interdependence, and mutual submission. The fourth-century Athanasian Creed reflects this, saying all persons of the trinity are "co-equal," "none is afore, or after other: none is greater, or less than another."[3]

Likewise, the church is most like God when it abandons hierarchy, power, and rank and emerges as a parallel community ordered by mutual submission, self-giving, sacrifice, and love. It means, as the apostle Paul put it, "There is neither Jew nor Greek, slave nor free, male nor female, for you are all one in Christ Jesus."[4] It means we should not structure our communities according to a corporate business model or a military chain-of-command model. It means, as Jesus said, "the rulers of the Gentiles lord it over them.... Not so with you."[5]

It means, I suppose, that we who are the church ought to treat each other the way Sean treated me.

SCRAPING COSMONAUTS OFF THE CEILING

O ur Soviet tour guide, whose name now escapes me, seemed especially eager to show us a building that was once a church. It was 1982. Ronald Reagan was in the White House. Lenin was still on display in his tomb. No one had yet heard of perestroika.

We followed our guide down a narrow street lined with bakeries and cafés. Stern old men in crisp military uniforms, World War II medals winking in the late summer sun, played chess at tables on the sidewalk and drank coffee so thick a spoon could stand up in it.

The whitewashed, golden-domed church filled a corner, noticeable only in that it was still kept up. (Most churches had been boarded up after the 1917 Bolshevik Revolution and had weathered sixty-five Russian winters by the time we saw them.) A tired-looking woman with two gold teeth and a cigarette affixed to her mouth sold tokens beneath a sign that, our guide explained, said Museum of Atheism.

With an enthusiasm he had not previously displayed, our guide took us into a room that had once been filled with the prayers and songs and scriptures voiced by generations of Russian Orthodox believers. Now it was filled with propaganda, wall-size posters with awkwardly composed English sentences telling why it is stupid to believe in God.

"Vill you look up, please?" our guide eagerly suggested, pointing upward to the inside of the dome. The sacred art that once adorned the ceiling had been painted over. In its place was a picture of the moon, sun, and other planets floating in the dark night of space. Two cosmonauts floated among the stars, their spacesuits proudly adorned with the letters CCCP in red and the hammer and sickle of the Soviet flag.

"Our cosmonauts have visited outer space," he said with a flourish. "And do you know vat they found? Notink. No God. Naturally. Soviet cosmonauts have proven the error of Western capitalist lie. God was not there."

Within a decade of our visit, Soviet Communism collapsed. The museums of atheism were closed and turned back into churches. Today the rivers of spirituality are surging in the former Soviet Union. New churches open every week.

Human beings need to worship; we are designed to be worshiping beings. If we cannot worship God, we will worship something else. When Saddam Hussein's statues began to topple across Iraq, I remembered that the Communists had decorated their cities with similar dictator décor—with statutes of Lenin on nearly every corner, pictures of Lenin on thousands of walls. The day we visited Lenin Square, the line to see Lenin's formaldehyde-preserved body was three hours long. We cannot *not* worship.

Yet we do not always know this.

"Secularism," wrote Alexander Schmemann, "is above all a negation of worship...it is the negation of man as a worshipping being."[1] There are many currents in life that negate us as worshiping beings, especially when we are young and life is full of hope and promise rather than regret and missed opportunities.

Sooner or later many of us feel the God-hunger reawaken. This spiritual reawakening may come as a vague dissatisfaction with pleasures that used to satisfy more fully, new thoughts about death and the afterlife, friends who begin sacred journeys and, surprisingly, leave you feeling left behind. What is awakening is a desire to worship. You are tired of looking at a sky painted over with spaceships and cosmonauts. You want to worship.

Jimmy and I sat in his office after several years of studying the bible together. I borrowed a page from my college Campus Crusade for Christ training and drew two circles on the whiteboard in his office. I drew a throne in the center of the first circle and put JHIII (my friend's initials) on the throne. Then I sketched the main priorities of his life, including his business, his marriage, his children, his health, his civic responsibilities. And I drew lines from those life priorities toward the throne.

"This is one way to live your life," I said. "You are at the center of your life. The priorities of your life revolve around your leadership of your own life."

I then drew a cross and placed it outside the circle. "Jesus is not on the throne. He is not leading your life. In this model you're the leader." Jimmy, chewing his pen and sensing two years of hard spiritual work was about to come to a head, nodded.

I then sketched a second circle on the board. I again drew a throne in the center of the circle and put the name JESUS CHRIST on the throne. I wrote JHIII beneath the throne, and put the same life priorities in the rest of the circle. Except this time these priorities revolved around Christ's leadership, not Jimmy's.

"Which circle best describes your life right now, Jimmy?" (Remember, we were two years into our relationship and had talked deeply about the spiritual life. I respected Jimmy and had earned the right to ask this very personal question.)

"The first one," he said, pointing to the circle with JHIII on the throne.

"Which circle do you want to represent your life?"

"The second one," he said, pointing to the circle with JESUS CHRIST on the throne.

And then Jimmy asked if he could draw up a contract and think about it over the weekend. I didn't have a good response. Nobody had ever asked me this before.

"This is important," he said. "I want to think about it…make sure I understand what I am doing." So Jimmy drew up a contract, took it home, talked to his family, and then met with me the next week to close the deal.

Jimmy decided to become a worshiper of God.

When we gather with our church for worship, we are declaring that we want to live in the second circle. We are saying with our mouths and our presence that God is God and we are not and that we want our lives to be ordered under his leadership, not our own.

Our word *worship* comes from an old English word *worthship,* which meant to pay homage to a worthy person, such as a king. We worship as a church because God is worth it. He is awesome. Unbelievable. Astounding. We worship to tell him that and, in the process, to remind ourselves that there are more than cosmonauts on the ceiling.

We worship God for who he is. "Ascribe to the LORD the glory due his name; worship the LORD in the splendor of his holiness," cried the psalmist.[2] We worship God because he is the creator of the world. "You are worthy," cried the twenty-four elders in John's Apocalypse, "our Lord and God, to receive glory and honor and power, for you created all things, and by your will they were created and have their being."[3] Above all, we worship him because he saved us. John records this hymn in his heavenly vision: "You are worthy to take the scroll and to open its seals, because you were slain, and with your blood you purchased men for God from every tribe and language and people and nation."[4]

We are designed for worship, and we need to worship the One who is worthy of our honor. That being said, our submission to God in worship is more important than *how* we worship. The church's styles of worship—liturgical, traditional, charismatic, or contemporary—are merely paint scrapers that help us strip away the cursed cosmonauts that cloud our vision of the divine so we can uncover the God who is waiting for us.

Our first attempts at worship are often tentative and awkward. We are saying nice things about a person we barely even know. As the God of our community becomes the God of our own daily life, our worship grows sweeter and becomes more personal. We love him and tell him so because he delivered us from sin through Christ's death on the cross but also because he delivered us from the smoldering ruins of such tragedies as divorce, sexual addiction, or shattered self-esteem.

Late in the twentieth century, worship burst from beneath the surface of the Soviet Union within hours of the fall of Communism. It came forth because humans are worshiping beings. Secularism, the negation of us as worshiping beings, ultimately fails. We cannot be fully human when there are still cosmonauts painted on the ceiling.

That's why the former Museum of Atheism is once again a church.

SAADIA'S GIFT

There is institutional racism in our city," Saadia says quietly. "I experience its cruelty every day."

Saadia is an attractive African American woman with a sunny smile and friendly eyes. She is sitting in an overstuffed chair in my office, talking about her new role with the Race Relations Center of East Tennessee. Her visit is timely. The previous weekend a young black man was shot and killed by two white police officers in the parking lot of Wiegel's, a gas station and convenience store. The police department said the officers' audiotape proved that the nineteen-year-old man had been warned prior to the fatal shot. The black community was not convinced, and the NAACP launched its own investigation.

The shooting was not the only news story featuring the NAACP in the Knoxville papers that week. Tucked away in the back of the A section of the papers, before the editorials and after the gossip, was a brief story about a hate-crime panel that was being established to investigate fifty racially motivated crimes whose victims lived in or around our community.

The day before the Wiegel's shooting, I taught a leadership retreat at Mount Zion Baptist Church, an African American congregation founded 124 years ago when the local Baptist church didn't want nonwhites among its members. Just before lunch, someone at the retreat mentioned Martin Luther King, Jr.'s, famous quote, "The eleven o'clock hour is the most segregated hour in America."

"We all know this is true," I admitted. "Your church is almost entirely black, and my church is almost entirely white." Heads nodded. I decided to take a risk, to try out an idea that I'd loosely clung to but wasn't sure I really believed.

"There is another way to think about this. God knows that people are naturally drawn toward people like themselves, people with the same cultural, ethnic, and economic backgrounds. Could it be that God doesn't mind it when we have churches with people who are like us, as long as we cooperate with churches of different kinds in our community?"

Silence hung over the room like a rain cloud, threatening to burst. My hosts were gracious. They didn't want to tell their guest what they really thought of his idea. "I'd really like to know what you think," I prodded. "Am I being too easy on myself?"

Silence. And then a hand rose. "Yes," replied a distinguished-looking gentlemen with a disarming smile, his eyes twinkling behind rimless glasses. "You are."

> You are a chosen people, a royal priesthood, a holy nation, a
> people belonging to God, that you may declare the praises of him
> who called you out of darkness into his wonderful light. Once
> you were not a people, but now you are the people of God.[1]

A royal priesthood, a holy nation, the church... The church, writes the apostle Peter, *is* the people of God. In the Old Testament, God calls a people to himself. They are Israel, the Hebrew nation. The people of God in the Old Testament are ethnically Jewish. Peter's words quoted above hint at the massive change that took place after Jesus walked the earth, teaching and modeling the life of God for us. After Jesus died and was resurrected, the "holy nation" mentioned by Peter included non-Jewish believers as well as Jewish believers. The people of God had a new look.

In 1871 an archaeologist named Charles Clermont-Ganneau was

digging in the ruins around the site of the Jerusalem temple that was destroyed in AD 70. He unearthed a broken piece of wall on which were Greek letters that posted this warning: "No foreigner is to enter the balustrade and embankment around the sanctuary. Whoever is caught will have himself to blame for his death which follows."[2] The inscription came from the five-foot-high wall of the temple that separated the outer court of the Gentiles from the inner court and sanctuary of the Jews. When the apostle Paul wrote to Christians living in Ephesus, he appeared to be referring to this barrier wall. He explained to the racially diverse Ephesian church that Jesus "has destroyed the barrier, the dividing wall of hostility,...to create in himself one new man out of the two."[3]

The people of God know no racial barriers. Jesus, in the ultimate act of selfless love and sacrifice, forgave us so that we can forgive the sins that wall us off from one another. The ancient world, like our own, was a divided world. Communities were fragmented on the basis of gender, class, status, and nationality. Christ's death changed all that—at least for the people of God, where there is now "neither Jew nor Greek, slave nor free, male nor female, for you are all one in Christ Jesus."[4] Paul's vision of a diverse new community in which everyone is on equal footing enabled him to write to a slave owner named Philemon, about his slave Onesimus, and suggest what was unthinkable in the culture of that day. Paul suggested that the slave owner "might have him [Onesimus] back for good—no longer as a slave, but better than a slave, as a dear brother."[5]

Meanwhile, back at Mount Zion Baptist Church, after my pathetic attempt to explain why it is somehow acceptable for the eleven o'clock hour on Sunday morning to be the most segregated hour of the week, we continued to discuss diversity and multicultural churches over lunch. When we finished lunch and began clearing the tables, an elderly woman approached me. "I was a part of a multicultural congregation" she said, smiling fondly at the memory. "It was the best experience of my life."

"Why?" I wanted to know. "Can you tell me about it?"

"It's the way God wanted it," she said. "That's why."

This is where I'm supposed to insert a moving story about how our church is now modeling before our fragmented city a loving, diverse, multicultural community. I can't tell that story because I don't have that story to tell. We're still pretty segregated come Sunday morning. We've tried to become more diverse, at least in small ways. We've exchanged choirs, we've built Habitat for Humanity homes together, and we've swapped youth groups with African American churches. I now consider a number of African American pastors good friends. We've had inter-racial discussion groups and read good books together. Usually, the groups begin well and then gradually peter out.

The problem, I've come to realize, is that I don't experience the problem in everyday life. The system works well for me. I don't suffer from institutional racism. I experience, and profit from, institutions created by white men that work very well for white men like me. Racism in my city? I don't see it because it doesn't touch my life.

Perhaps that is why our efforts at becoming the multicultural faith community that Paul describes are so difficult, even frightening to many on my side of the wall. If I get too close to Saadia, close in a way that goes beyond building a house together or enjoying each other's worship services, I might have to feel what she feels when she's being followed by an undercover detective in a department store. Racism in my city? Saadia sees it, feels it, lives it. If I really get to know her, I'll have to see it and feel it and know it.

Saadia and I have a pleasant conversation in my office while a quiet May rain washes the streets beneath my fourth-floor window. Would I be willing to join her in a study circle on Fridays? she wants to know, explaining that this would be a five-week small group in which blacks and whites openly and candidly share their feelings about race. Maybe, she says, if we really understood one another, good would come of it.

I feel anxious about this. I feel I will be exposed as a failure and a fraud. I feel suddenly very busy, especially on Fridays from ten till noon. Yet Saadia is my friend. I trust her. I believe in her vision. She has courage to go out every day and do what she does at the Race Relations Center.

A verse comes to mind, a snapshot of heaven. It's from John's Apocalypse. The four living creatures and the twenty-four elders are singing a song to Jesus:

> You are worthy to take the scroll
> and to open its seals,
> because you were slain,
> and with your blood you purchased men for God
> from every tribe and language and people and nation.
> You have made them to be a kingdom and priests to serve our
> God,
> and they will reign on the earth.[6]

The new community God is forming in the church today is a multicultural community filled with men, women, and children from every tribe, language, and nation.

"Yes," I tell Saadia—but not bravely. "I would like to be part of that group."

Later, as I reflect on the meeting, I am dimly aware of God's presence and of something good but not safe being birthed. A black woman's courage has touched a white man's fear. Another piece of the wall has fallen down.

FATHER PANELOUX'S SERMON

Father Paneloux's first sermon in plague-ridden Oran brings little comfort to the terrified townspeople who have filled the cathedral hungry for a word of hope.

"Calamity has come on you, my brethren, and, my brethren, you deserved it," the stocky priest thunders from his pulpit before gathering up Old Testament metaphors and hurling them like spears into the hearts of his listeners. The plague, Father Paneloux concludes, "reveals the will of God in action, unfailingly transforming evil into good."[1]

Dr. Bernard Rieux, the physician who saves many in Oran from the plague, cannot agree. Months later the priest and the doctor meet at the bedside of a dying boy.

Rieux swung around on him [Father Paneloux] fiercely.

"Ah! That child, anyhow, was innocent, and you know it as well as I do."…

"I understand," Paneloux said in a low voice. "That sort of thing is revolting because it passes our human understanding. But perhaps we should love what we cannot understand."

Rieux straightened up slowly. He gazed at Paneloux.…

"No, Father. I've a very different idea of love. And until my dying day I shall refuse to love a scheme of things in which children are put to torture."[2]

The church does not come off well in Albert Camus' novel *The Plague*. Little comfort is found in the pews of the Cathedral of Oran. Sadly, Father Paneloux is not a mere straw man. He represents a twisted expression of Christianity that often creeps into our churches: a fatalistic, overly passive way of viewing the human predicament that sees suffering either as justly deserved punishment or a glorious gift, or both.

However, we don't detect such a scheme in the teaching or ministry of Jesus. Far from passively accepting suffering as God's punishment or as an aid to spiritual growth, Jesus confronts suffering at every turn, and he urges his community to do the same. "When Jesus came into Peter's house, he saw Peter's mother-in-law lying in bed with a fever. He touched her hand and the fever left her."[3]

Jesus heals the sick because he has compassion on hurting people. "Jesus went through all the towns and villages, teaching in their synagogues, preaching the good news of the kingdom and healing every disease and sickness," Matthew records in his gospel. "When he saw the crowds, he had compassion on them."[4]

The church carries on Christ's healing ministry in response to words James wrote to the churches under his care a generation after Christ's ascension: "Is any one of you sick? He should call the elders of the church to pray over him and anoint him with oil in the name of the Lord."[5]

We pray for healing because Christ prayed for healing and told his disciples to do the work of healing the sick. Sometimes God's answers to these prayers are dramatic, miraculous, even breathtaking. Other times the healing comes not in a miracle but in the grace to bear wounds that do not heal.

Camus' dramatic novel ends with the citizens of Oran celebrating having survived their ordeal by dancing in the streets. Dr. Rieux, however, "remembered that such joy is always imperiled…that the plague bacillus never dies or disappears for good; that it can lie dormant for years in furniture and linen-chests; that it bides its time in bedrooms, cellars, trunks and bookshelves; and that perhaps the day would come when, for the bane and enlightening of men, it would rouse up its rats again and send them forth to die in a happy city."[6]

Our world is like that. Any healing we experience in this life is partial and temporary. But it is still healing, and it is still real even if the healing is simply the grace to bear suffering with dignity and hope.

The church has always worked to relieve suffering. When a great plague struck in the second century, caravans and wagons hauled the dead from cities. One of every four people in the Roman Empire died. A century later, a plague swept across the Roman world that took five thousand lives a day. Seventy percent of the citizens of Alexandria, Egypt, perished. At the height of this second epidemic, Alexandria's bishop, Dionysius, celebrated the church's heroic service to her neighbors in his Easter letter, commending them because they had "showed unbounded love and loyalty, never sparing themselves…. Heedless of danger, they took charge of the sick, attending to their every need and ministering to them in Christ."[7]

Today, the AIDS epidemic threatens to wipe out the lives of one hundred million people. The church is responding through people like Rich Stearns, a fifty-two-year-old Wharton Business School graduate. Stearns was earning $800,000 a year as the CEO of Lenox, a luxury china company. He and his wife had five kids, a company Jaguar, a dog named Snickers, and a ten-bedroom house in the Philadelphia suburbs.

Then a headhunter called, suggesting that Stearns consider becoming the next president of World Vision, an international organization that helps the church serve some of the world's neediest people. Stearns said he wasn't qualified and wasn't interested. God evidently thought he was.

Five months later he had quit his job, taken a 75 percent pay cut, and moved his family to a Seattle suburb so he could head the work of World Vision. Two months later he traveled to Uganda. "I'd been traveling to places like Florence and Paris with the china business. I wasn't sure what to expect in Uganda," he says.

Stearns's staffers took him to a village where thousands of orphans live without parents because of AIDS. Three brothers, ages thirteen, eleven, and ten, particularly stand out in his memory. "The oldest boy's name—I don't think coincidentally—was Richard. Same as my name," Stearns told a reporter. "I think that was God's way of showing me, this is where I am calling you."[8]

Under Stearns's leadership, World Vision has made fighting AIDS its number-one priority, launching a public awareness campaign, sending lobbyists to Washington, and spending ninety billion dollars in African countries that have high rates of HIV.

"My staff calls me the weeping president," Stearns admitted to a group of potential donors. "I can't talk about what I saw in Uganda without crying."[9]

In the Middle Ages, paintings of Christ often depicted him amidst plague victims, sometimes weeping. As Rich Stearns has discovered, that's exactly where those who follow Jesus belong.

POLITICS AS SHALOM
MAKING

P olitics is building community with strangers."

Chris Woodhull, a respected community leader in his early for-
ties, is running for a seat on the Knoxville City Council. When he's not
campaigning, Chris is the executive director of TribeOne, a faith-based
nonprofit organization that works with teenagers affiliated with gangs.
I'm interested in listening to Chris's views on the church's role in politics
because I know he shares my ambivalence toward much of what has
passed for church-based political action.

Just prior to our conversation, I pull a book off the shelf, and a letter from a conservative Christian political group falls out. The letter is
written in red, white, and blue ink with whole paragraphs set in boldface
type. It features lines such as "the stakes are incredibly high" and "we
must fight." The boldface words are underlined just to make sure I don't
miss them. The letter ends with an appeal for a "victory gift" to support
voter guides that will tell the faithful who the approved Christian candidates are. None of the "approved" candidates is a Democrat, by the way.
How did the gospel become connected with the Republican Party?

The posturing of the political left is just as annoying. That great suck-
ing sound that so many church watchers heard in the last quarter of the
past century was the sound of millions of spiritually famished Christians

exiting their churches because they didn't want to hear another sermon on global warming or nuclear disarmament.

At least liberals and conservatives have tried to relate their faith to their politics. Other Christians have opted out of the political process, retreating to Christian ghettos while they await the setting of the moral sun. That strikes me as gutless.

So what am I left with? I don't want to be liberal, conservative, or gutless. I've been reading a book that calls for a "third way" that arises "out of a deepening hunger among many to find a…'spiritual politics' beyond the old polarized options of Left and Right, liberal and conservative."[1] I share this hunger for a third way. I sense Chris does too.

"What has the campaign been like?" I ask Chris.

"Frightening," he answers. "Running for office is a spectacle. But it is a gift, too."

"A gift?"

"It has opened up rooms inside of me that have been locked. When we go through things like this, we see what's inside us." The grueling political campaign has become a means of spiritual formation for Chris—a crucible that refines him. I had never before thought of the refining process as a reason for the church to enter the public square, but it's a good one: We grow spiritually when we bring faith to bear on issues that are crucial to the well-being of society.

Chris and I talk about his calling into politics. He recalls a father who loved JFK, a year spent in Washington working for a think tank, an African American friend named Danny, now deceased, who ran for office as an act of worship. Chris senses that I am hoping for something a little more dramatic, but he doesn't go there.

"Modern Christianity is too utopian," he says. "The Christian life is really about the ordinary, not the ideal. Place is important. The land is important. Politics is putting morality into practice. It's a pragmatic dealing with life in a particular place, a community, our community."

"What is a community?"

"A community is a place that supports our growth and wholeness. A community holds us, helps us feel alive."

"And the goal of Christian politics, then, is…?"

"To build a place that works for everybody, a real place, a community with social equity, a community where everyone has economic access, a community that is economically sound and livable."

The Hebrew prophets, when they dreamed of healthy communities, described their vision with the ancient word *shalom*. Shalom means "harmony, wholeness, completion, things as they should be." Sometimes our bibles translate *shalom* as "peace," but it is a much fuller word than that. In fact, a vast project to restore shalom to the world unfolds across the pages of scripture. God creates the world. Initially it enjoys shalom. Then sin destroys shalom and introduces alienation. The Old Testament is the story of God's attempt to restore the shalom of Eden. The angels at Christ's birth sing that he has come to bring shalom. The apostle Paul tells us that Christ's death recovered shalom. John's Apocalypse foresees the restoration of shalom on all the earth as the goal of history.

Shalom is a real place that works for everybody. "Seek the peace and prosperity [shalom] of the city," the prophet Jeremiah said.[2] This is the purpose of politics. This is why Chris is running for a seat on the city council. This is why the church must be involved in politics. Politics is a tool for shalom making.

I find myself puzzling over the ramifications of what Chris has said. I hope he wins the election, partly because I can't wait to see how reporters handle him and partly because I think we need people like him in office. I tell him this before we part.

Our conversation ends with glimpses of insight and invitations to hope, but no coherent theory of Christian political involvement. I am both moved and mildly frustrated. Perhaps politicians who are poets are uniquely qualified to serve as guides along the political road less traveled. An hour later my phone rings. Chris wants to say one more thing. Perhaps *now* I'll get a great sound bite to wrap this essay around.

"I've been reading a speech Václav Havel gave on politics at New York University. Listen to this," he begins. Quoting the Czech poet and president, Chris continues: "'Politics should be principally the domain of people with a heightened sense of responsibility and a heightened sense of the mysterious complexity of *being*.'"[3]

I write frantically on my notepad.

"Isn't that beautiful?" he asks.

Yes, I tell him. It is.

NEW SCIENCE AND THE
NEW COMMUNITY

One of the first rules of writing is "write about what you know." I'm about to break that rule. I don't know much about science. When I'm browsing through a bookstore and accidentally pick up a book with words such as *quark* and *photon* in it, my mind grows fuzzy and I feel faint. Only another cup of coffee and a few moments of serenely browsing among the novels can save the day.

Someone has said that a big part of wisdom is knowing what you don't know. I know I don't know much about science, but I know that those who do know something say that science experienced a massive revolution in the twentieth century. The results of this revolution are only now trickling down to people like me who buy *Physics for Dummies* and still don't get it. Here's what really smart people are saying…

Physicist Stephen Hawking asked the question, "Is the end in sight for theoretical physics?" at a 1980 lecture at Cambridge University. His answer? Yes, it is. A new science is emerging out of the old. James Gleick, in his national bestseller *Chaos: Making a New Science,* believes three scientific revolutions took place in the past century resulting in three new theories that radically transform the way we think about how life works.[1]

More than fifty years ago, bizarre and stunning new ideas about space and time, mind and matter, erupted within the scientific community. In the first quarter of the twentieth century, two momentous theories were proposed: the theory of relativity and quantum theory. From them sprang most of twentieth-century physics. But the new physics soon revealed more than simply a better model of a physical world. Physicists began to realize that their discoveries demanded a radical reformation of the most fundamental aspects of reality:

> The fruits of this revolution are only now starting to be plucked by philosophers and theologians. Many ordinary people, too, searching for a deeper meaning behind their lives, find their beliefs about the world very much in tune with the new physics.[2]

My first brief encounters with the new physics in the early eighties came in offhanded comments professors made about Einstein's theory of relativity's proving that all truth was relative. This threatened my belief in a God who revealed true truths. I didn't understand what the theory of relativity meant, and I wasn't about to take a physics course to find out, fearing it would ruin my GPA. At a deeper level, math and science scared me. I had trouble understanding the concepts, and I was afraid of what I might find if I pressed in too deeply. For nearly twenty years I pleaded ignorance and thought about other things.

Then I read a book by Brian McLaren called *A New Kind of Christian*. The book describes the spiritual crisis of Dan Poole, a thirty-something minister whose faith is crumbling under the weight of nagging intellectual questions and the pressure he feels not to ask them. Neo, a former Episcopal priest from Jamaica with a PhD in the history of science, serves as Dan's spiritual guide. Neo helps Dan discover that science is not the enemy of faith. In fact, Neo informs his young friend, the new discoveries of science actually support faith.[3]

As a pastor who has wrestled with many of the questions Dan Poole has, I connected with the book on many levels and wanted to know more.

A Web-site search led me to *www.emergentvillage.com*, a conversation among leaders interested in exploring the postmodern church. Several more clicks to related links led me to bibliographies that included books proposing that the insights of the new science may help us better understand life in the new community of faith. I began collecting books, slowly reading and looking for intersection points.

I was surprised to discover that scientists and theologians both sense they are in the midst of a massive thought revolution. Scientists say we are leaving behind the world of Isaac Newton, whose laws of physics governed the scientific world for more than two hundred years. Newton saw the world as a great machine: predictable, regular, quietly ticking away like a giant clock. The universe is run by observable natural laws, Newton thought. Discover the laws, and you learn how the universe works. Eventually, we would learn all the laws, come up with a Theory of Everything, and therefore control the universe. There is no mystery or magic in how life works: All is explained by laws discovered or yet to be discovered.

Newton's paradigm appealed to our innate desire to control things. The Enlightenment led us to believe that when we accumulated enough knowledge, we could set things right. Finally, things would work the way we *wanted* them to. Then Newtonian physics began to disintegrate when scientists discovered that the world within the atom was a very strange world. It shares very little in common with the orderly, law-abiding universe that Newton described. Scientists, who formerly used the metaphor of the machine to describe the nature of reality, began to find new metaphors. One described the world as "a vast porridge of being"; another as "dynamic patterns continually changing into one another—the continuing dance of energy." This new world is one where "everything is connected like a vast network of interference patterns." An astronomer suggests that "the universe begins to look more like a great thought than a great machine."[4]

I don't pretend to understand it, and even leading scientists admit that this sounds pretty weird. Yet even a science-challenged person like me can sense intuitively that the world the new physicists are describing is not unlike the strange world of the Spirit we find described in the bible. The universe is not a machine; it is a living system, an interconnected network of relationships, a great web of life.

I was looking for user-friendly books on the theory of relativity, quantum physics, and chaos theory at a bookstore one summer afternoon when I came across Margaret Wheatley's book *Leadership and the New Science*. As I flipped through the pages, a chapter heading caught my eye: "Newtonian Organizations in a Quantum Age."

A few paragraphs into the chapter, Wheatley writes, "It is interesting to note just how Newtonian most organizations are,"[5] meaning that we have treated organizations like machines because we thought the world worked that way. We focus on rules, plans, procedures, measurements, control, authority, responsibility, and linear cause-and-effect thinking because these are how the machinery of organizations works.

I'd found another intersection point: Many churches seem "Newtonian." They become vast impersonal institutions, religious machines that thrive on routine, predictability, and management by objective. I've often been discouraged when life in the community of God seems more managed than mystical, more organized than organic, more controlled than chaotic. Why? Perhaps it's because we've been infected with the virus of Newtonian physics—a way of thinking about life, and especially life in the faith community, as a machine instead of a mystical body.

Later that evening, with a highlighting pen in hand, I read the first paragraphs over again and scribbled some questions on a piece of paper. *What does an organization look like when it is shaped by the insights of the new science?* I read on in Wheatley's book and never found *the* answer. I did, however, find numerous clues and hints that pointed toward a way people can be together that is less machinelike and more interconnected, interwoven, participatory, and mysterious. Organizations that grasp their identity as interconnected relational networks and not machines, Wheatley concludes, will thrive.

She and other authors writing on the subject use a kaleidoscope of words to describe the way new science perceives life: fluid, nonlinear, networked, webbed, interdependent, chaotic yet orderly, participatory, interactive, responsive, holistic, reproductive. These words resonate with what I know to be the church.

Reading is often a mystical experience for me. I experience God's guidance as I read books, leading me down a winding trail vaguely marked by ideas and authors. Einstein and Werner Heisenberg's discoveries regarding the interconnectedness of life remind me of an ancient definition of the church found in one of the apostle Paul's letters to the church at Corinth: "The body is a unit, though it is made up of many parts; and though all its parts are many, they form one body."[6] The church is a living system, a network of interwoven relationships. The church is not a machine or an institution. The church is alive, a living cell, organic, chaotic, nonlinear.

Let's walk down the trail a little farther. One of the main differences between the old science and the new science is what scientists look at. Old science looks primarily at the individual parts that make up the machine. New science looks primarily at the whole, how the entire system works together. This holistic view of life is also called systems thinking. One of the first books that made systems thinking known to the public was Peter Senge's *The Fifth Discipline*.

> Systems thinking is a discipline for seeing wholes. It is a framework for seeing interrelationships rather than things, for seeing patterns of change rather than static "snapshots." It is a set of general principles—distilled over the course of the twentieth century, spanning fields as diverse as the physical and social sciences, engineering, and management.... And systems thinking is sensibility—for the subtle

interconnectedness that gives living systems their unique character.... Systems thinking is the cornerstone of how learning organizations think about their world.[7]

Which brings me to a story about my kids. Even babies get bored.
Unable to enjoy the finer childhood pleasures in store for them down the
road, babies lie on their backs and slobber. They also like to look at
things. When our kids were pre-Nintendo, we bought them a mobile at
a garage sale and hung it over the crib. You probably looked at one when
you were a baby. A dozen little blue and red airplanes hung from a string
attached to a plastic bridge that covered the crib. Early on, our kids just
stared at the planes and slobbered. We knew they had hit a development
milestone when they could reach up, hit one of the planes, and then slobber. A funny thing happens when you hit one plane in a mobile: All the
planes move. This keeps the kid interested for as long as the planes move.
This is also a good picture of what happens in a system. Every part of the
system is connected with every other part; so if you touch one part,
you've touched every part.

In the film *Bruce Almighty*, Jim Carrey plays Bruce Nolan, a dis-
gruntled television reporter who is passed over for the top anchor spot
and becomes furious with God for refusing to answer his prayers. God,
played by Morgan Freeman, gets tired of Bruce's complaining and gives
him the powers to be God for a while. Bruce uses his new powers self-
ishly at first, and then he begins paying attention to the millions of prayer
requests flooding in. He decides to answer yes to every one of them.
Thousands of people win the lottery, so the prize for each winner is almost
nothing, economies begin to fall apart, chaos reigns. Bruce learns a quick
lesson about systems: Touch one part, and you touch it all.

The apostle Paul envisions the church as a living, interconnected
system when he writes, "If one part suffers, every part suffers with it; if
one part is honored, every part rejoices with it."[8] Sometimes we fail to

understand the interconnected nature of the church, and we put into place practices and policies that contradict one another. For example, a church might truly value giving to the poor but erects a building so expensive that all extra money goes to pay off the mortgage. Or a pastor might tell the people they should get to know their neighbors while also telling them to be at church several times a week. It's not possible to do both.[9]

What does the new science mean for the church? Here are some questions regarding the church as an organism, a whole, versus the old assumptions about the church as an organization or an institution.

- If reality is like a thought, could it be God's thought?
- Could the new community of faith somehow be the thought of God, expressed in a living spiritual family?
- How do power and control function in a network? What types of new leadership styles are required?
- If the church is an interconnected network, is there any hierarchy that remains? Is hierarchy in the church Newtonian? Is the traditional way of thinking about gender roles also Newtonian, a holdover from an old way of thinking about life as linear and ranked, an artificial hierarchy that doesn't apply to an organism?
- Chaos theory says order comes out of chaos. What does this tell us about chaotic times in church life and how we should lead and live through them?
- The new science says that reality is participatory: We somehow influence reality by observing it. What does this say about the prayer life of the faith community? What does this say about the community's discernment of God's will? What does it say about the church's impact on the outside community?
- How would the community's life together be different if we conceived our community as a network or an interconnected relational web instead of an institution?

- Scientists, even those without religious faith, are speaking of the mystery and magic of the universe. Does the new science re-introduce the mystical into our understanding of the church's nature?
- If all of life is an interconnected web, how is the church connected to the ecological environment?
- If all of life is an interconnected web, how is the local church connected to other churches?
- If all of life is an interconnected web, how is the church connected to different faith communities?

These are the questions I ask as I stand at the clearing. Maybe you will answer them.

ON NOT LEAVING IT TO THE HOLLOW MEN

During the summer of 1972, all the best game shows were pre-empted by something called Watergate. I was furious. What right did they have to shove aside Bob Barker and *The Price Is Right* for a bunch of middle-aged guys in dark suits arguing about a break-in at the Watergate Building? Two years later I was snapping towels at other guys at a swim meet when Richard Nixon resigned. I had just made my best time in the fifty-yard backstroke, and that seemed more important at the moment. I didn't realize then that the Watergate scandal signaled the collapse of America's trust in authority.

Pre-Watergate Americans tended to trust the government. Post-Watergate Americans still have not regained a sense of trust. Dag, a character in the novel *Generation X*, reflects this distrust of leaders when he resigns his job and tells off his Boomer boss:

> Do you really think we enjoy hearing about your brand-new
> million-dollar home when we can barely afford to eat Kraft
> Dinner sandwiches in our own grimy little shoe boxes when
> we're pushing thirty? A home you won in a genetic lottery, I
> might add, sheerly by dint of your having been born at the right
> time in history? You'd last about ten minutes if you were my age

these days, Martin. And I have to endure pinheads like you rusting above me for the rest of my life, always grabbing for the best
bit of cake first and then putting a barbed-wire fence around the
rest. You really make me sick.[1]

Spiritual communities are not immune to the abuse of a leader's
power, as the headlines all too frequently remind us. "But you are not to
be like that," Jesus reminds us.[2] Jesus supplied leaders to help the community become mature—to relate in healthy ways and to fulfill its mission.[3] When Paul, an apostle and first-century missionary, formed new
communities of faith across present-day Turkey and Macedonia, he
quickly appointed leadership teams to guide them.[4]

The New Testament churches were a loosely connected network of
communities held together by a common faith in the same Lord. Leadership was decentralized: Many of the leaders led many networks of
many churches, and no one leader led them all. Paul and an early associ-
ate, Barnabas, appointed elders in every church, not just one elder. Paul
spoke of a plurality of elders leading the church in Ephesus, telling a
young pastor named Titus to appoint elders (plural) in every town.[5]

To use a precarious metaphor, the early church was organized like
today's al Qaeda terrorist networks. Contrary to popular opinion, there
is no "one great leader" coordinating all activity from the top down in
such networks. Instead, various cells within the network are interconnected like a spider web. The network has little hierarchy, and there are
multiple leaders. Decision making and operations are decentralized. Each
cell has the freedom to act without a clumsy process of seeking the go-
ahead from up top. Instead of forced unity dictated by a single leader, the
network is held together by passionately shared ideology. A government
report issued after the September 11 attacks described these networks as
"dispersed organizations, small groups, and individuals who communicate, coordinate, and conduct their campaigns in an internetted manner,

often without a precise central command."[6] This sounds like the New Testament church!

The interconnected network of churches we find described in the New Testament does not stay that way for long. By the end of the first century, the church had begun to copy the hierarchical organizational patterns of the Roman Empire. Bishops appeared in the cities, overseeing the churches. The bishop of Rome soon became the bishop with the highest rank. Other bishops were expected to give him the final say in church matters. Plural leadership teams were replaced with priests who alone could dispense the sacraments. Leadership became highly centralized and hierarchical. Grace flowed from the top down, from God to the pope (the bishop of Rome) to the other bishops to the priests and, finally, to the people.

Today, however, parts of the church are returning to the network model seen in the churches of the first century. Denominations are gradually fading away, while networks of autonomous, like-minded churches are springing up. Collaboration and partnership are valued ahead of denominational affiliation or identical statements of faith. More than once a pastor friend has said to me, "I feel more in common with the other churches in my city than with my own denomination."

Today's churches appear to be returning to a network model—a system at odds with the hierarchical leadership model of the military and the corporate world. This trend, and it's a healthy one, presents a tremendous challenge, however. The old ways of leadership don't work anymore. Traditional leaders have no idea how to "lead" a network. How do you lead a web? We are living amidst a leadership transition—some would say a revolution. As Bill Easum puts it, "What does leadership mean when the old rules are disappearing and new ones have not yet emerged?"[7]

When my high-school-age daughter reaches adulthood, it's likely that she will find herself in a church that has transitioned from hierarchical leadership back to the New Testament model of networked congregations. Suppose she becomes a leader in her church? How will she lead? Following are a few predictions.

Her leadership will be more Frodo Baggins than George Patton. Frodo and the assorted elves, hobbits, dwarfs, wizards, women, and men who make up the fellowship of the ring share leadership depending on the particular challenge they face. Sometimes Gimli's axe is called for, sometimes Aragorn's arrow, sometimes Boromir's sword, sometimes Gandalf's wizardry, sometimes Sam's encouragement, sometimes Frodo's dogged perseverance. Frodo carries the vision (the ring), but the burden of leadership is shared equally. This is the spirit of Paul's words to the Christians in Corinth: "The eye cannot say to the hand, 'I don't need you!' And the head cannot say to the feet, 'I don't need you!'... You are the body of Christ, and each one of you is a part of it."[8]

The poet T. S. Eliot described the leaders of his day as "hollow men"—leaders without character. The apostle Paul seemed especially concerned that the leaders of his young churches not be "hollow men." "Now the [leader] must be above reproach...," he instructed his protégé Timothy, who was starting new congregations in the city of Ephesus. Then Paul continued the list describing the inner life of a church leader. He must be "temperate, self-controlled, respectable, hospitable, able to teach, not given to drunkenness, not violent but gentle, not quarrelsome, not a lover of money. He must manage his own family well and see that his children obey him with proper respect.... He must also have a good reputation with outsiders."[9]

A wise Christian leader, Leighton Ford, calls this "leading from within." My daughter, should she be called upon to provide leadership for her faith community, will be concerned about the soul of her leadership. Networks are close-knit relational communities, not impersonal bureaucracies. When the layers of middle management evaporate and the gap between leader and led shrinks, relationships matter more and character counts. Her personal spirituality will be more important to her leadership role than her leadership skills or management techniques. She will lead from her prayers, she will lead from her doubts, and she will lead from her scars. She will lead from the mystery and toward the chaos that is life in the Spirit.

Edwin Friedman, the rabbi who was the first to apply systems theory to life in spiritual communities, defines a leader as a "non-anxious presence" in the community's family system.[10] My daughter will likely have a better grasp than I do of her church as a family system. If she emerges into leadership within the family system, she will need to learn to be present with other members of the system. Her leadership must be engaged, caring, connected, and concerned. But being present is not enough. Her presence must be paired with a clear sense of who she is and who she is not, where she ends and where the community begins. She must be close but also separate, different, distinct; nonanxious when fear or anxiety grips the community.

Should my daughter become part of a new generation of leaders who learn how to lead networks instead of hierarchies, she will not be learning alone. A story on the front page of the *Washington Post* carried a headline that asked, "Can the Marines Survive a Shift from Hierarchies to Networks?" Reporter Joel Garreau interviewed marine commanders who are trying to make the shift. Garreau joined a military game in which nineteen-year-old marine corporals hit the beaches with computers strapped to their chests so they could network communications with every other soldier on the field, in the air, and even back at headquarters. A young soldier, networked directly with the entire unit, now has the capacity to call down more firepower with a click of a computer key than an entire command unit was able to summon during World War II.

"This exercise is not only about how technology will transform the way the Marines fight, but also how they think about who they are," Garreau reflects. "It is about one of the big ideas of the Information Age—

the rise of human networks and the fall of hierarchies—and about how this idea might reshape a traditional, top-down military organization."[11]

The war game over, Garreau wondered, "Can [the marines] transform themselves into a human network—an instantaneously reacting, self-organizing swarm that can metamorphose on the fly? Can they do this without tearing apart the essence of their organization?"[12]

Those who embrace the challenge of leadership in the emerging church are about to find out.

THE PEOPLE OF THE LIE

Arthur Miller's play *The Crucible* opens in the upper bedroom of the Reverend Samuel Parris, a minister in Salem, Massachusetts. It is the spring of 1692, and the devil is at work. Miller wants to recount the story to a nation swept up in the frenzy of the anti-Communist McCarthy hearings. The play opened at New York's Martin Beck Theater on January 22, 1953.

In the play a number of girls have been discovered dancing and playing and conjuring spirits in the forest with a West Indian slave named Tituba. As the weakest members in a stern theocratic village, the girls know that death is the penalty for dabbling in the occult. They begin to deflect the blame by falsely accusing their neighbors of practicing witchcraft. Before long the town is whipped into a frenzy, and the jail is filled with innocent people.[1]

The actual story is even grimmer in some of its details than Miller's play. The lines between church and state had blurred until they were invisible in the Salem of the late seventeenth century. God and government worked hand in hand. Salem's Puritans practiced church discipline, in which citizens/church members—the same thing in the Salem of 1692—were put out of the community when found guilty of serious sins. The excommunication was either by death or exile. Everyone in Salem was part of the one congregational church that joined with the government to prosecute crime and sin. Eventually, nineteen women would be hanged for witchcraft.

Twenty years after the hanging of innocent people, the congregation that called for the executions chose to rescind the victims' excommunications, but only after the government ordered it. Certain farms that had belonged to the victims were left to ruin, and for nearly a century no one would buy them or live on them.

Against the backdrop of the abuses of spiritual power chronicled on the pages of church history, reflective Christians are often troubled by practices such as "excommunication" or "church discipline." The terms themselves seem like anachronisms from the Middle Ages.

The church as I've tried to describe it in this book is an inclusive, welcoming place; a community of tolerance, grace, and forgiveness. Yet we are also a community that wrestles with a sacred text that sometimes says things that don't make sense to us. Take, for example, the New Testament teachings the Puritans used to support the witch trials.

If your brother sins against you, go and show him his fault, just between the two of you. If he listens to you, you have won your brother over. But if he will not listen, take one or two others along, so that "every matter may be established by the testimony of two or three witnesses." If he refuses to listen to them, tell it to the church; and if he refuses to listen even to the church, treat him as you would a pagan or a tax collector.[2]

It is actually reported that there is sexual immorality among you, and of a kind that does not occur even among pagans: A man has his father's wife. And you are proud! Shouldn't you rather have been filled with grief and have put out of your fellowship the man who did this?… When you are assembled in the name of our Lord Jesus and I am with you in spirit, and the power of our Lord

Jesus is present, hand this man over to Satan, so that the sinful nature may be destroyed and his spirit saved on the day of the Lord.[3]

A dozen objections immediately come to mind. Who am I to judge anybody? Doesn't Jesus tell us to forgive? Isn't the church supposed to be a place where all are welcome? Aren't these words just harsh holdovers from an ancient, unforgiving world?

The problem with these objections is that the texts calling for the removal of certain kinds of people from the community appear side by side with texts that call us to forgive and support one another as we struggle with sin. While we may have trouble imagining a community that is both forgiving and boundaried, the New Testament writers evidently did not.

Every living being has an inside and an outside. Animal communities have protective boundaries that nourish the good and deflect the bad. When danger threatens musk oxen, for example, they gather in a circle with heads and horns turned outward, protecting their vulnerable calves in the center of the circle. Human communities have insides and outsides as well. Our laws protect what is good and keep out what is bad so the community can enjoy peace.

A headline in this morning's newspaper declares, "Killer's Penalty Stiffened. Judge Tacks Twenty-Five Years onto Sentence for Attempted Murder of Wisconsin Woman." The article explains that Criminal Court Judge Richard Baumgartner had the opportunity to let convicted murderer Howard Thomas serve his sentences concurrently with the hope of parole but opted to put Thomas behind bars for the rest of his life. "He is a dangerous person with little or no regard for human life," Baumgartner said, and effectively removed the murderer from our community.[4]

Church discipline is the removal of a dangerous person from the faith community.

Sadly, even the most loving families can find it necessary to ask a family member to leave. A woman I know had a husband who wanted to carry on an affair while remaining married to her. Fearful of losing him, she tolerated his betrayal for a season and looked the other way. Counseling helped her see that her enabling of her husband's unfaithfulness was not good for either of them. She told him he had to choose. He could either live faithfully within the family or live irresponsibly outside of it. He couldn't do both.

No one wants to reproduce the horrors of the Salem Witch Trials. But anarchy isn't the answer either. There are bad people in the world. We shouldn't allow them to roam like wolves through our community, destroying the flock. Jesus, speaking of such people, warns, "The wolf attacks the flock and scatters it."[5]

A man came to our church once. I'll call him Dave. He said all the right things and seemed to believe the right things. We were a new church, our crowds were swelling, and our leaders were overworked. We gave Dave authority in our community without first getting to know him. Within a few months we noticed a troubling pattern. Dave left broken relationships in his wake wherever he went. Couples Dave spent time with began to turn on each other. Healthy teams Dave joined became suspicious and mistrusting. People who were exposed to Dave as a teacher became cynical of other leaders in our church.

Anyone who confronted Dave left the confrontation bewildered. His responses were always sprinkled with touches of bible verses and a dash of self-righteousness. You left your meetings with Dave wondering if it wasn't really *you* who had the problem. Everything about the man was confusing. Later I discovered from other pastors that Dave had left a trail of destruction in their churches, too.

Years after this man left our community, a friend lent me M. Scott Peck's book *People of the Lie*. "Evil," Peck writes, "is that force, residing either inside or outside of human beings, that seeks to kill life."[6]

Peck goes on to argue that in rare cases people actually *become* evil. Everyone sins, Peck argues, but evil people refuse to admit this. They cannot and will not face the reality of their own sin. "The evil hate the light—the light of goodness that shows them up, the light of scrutiny that exposes them, the light of truth that penetrates their deception."[7]

In psychologist Carl Jung's terms, evil people refuse to face the shadow, the dark side of their own personalities.[8] Unwilling and unable to confront their own failures, they reflect all problems onto those who confront them. Thus, their relationships are covered with a cloud of confusion, "another reaction the evil frequently engenders in us," according to Peck.[9] He continues, "Describing an encounter with an evil person, one woman wrote, it was 'as if I'd suddenly lost my ability to think.' Once again, this reaction is quite appropriate. The evil are 'the people of the lie,' deceiving others as they also build layer upon layer of self-deception."[10]

Peck's observations and insights helped me understand people like Dave. He also gave me some insight into how church discipline functions in a loving community. Church discipline is for those we could rightly call the People of the Lie. Ninety-nine percent of us are merely sinners. We struggle with sin, and we know it. When a friend confronts us, we own what is ours to own, say our apologies, ask for forgiveness, and move on. Occasionally we get stuck in the process and bring a wise third party into the conversation. In this sense we are "disciplining" ourselves all the time.

The spirit of these gentle conversations is captured in Paul's letter to Christians living in Galatia: "Brothers, if someone is caught in a sin, you who are spiritual should restore him gently. But watch yourself, or you also may be tempted."[11] The church's simple process for solving relational conflicts—go to each other and talk it out; and if that doesn't work find a mediator—solves most relational problems in the community. Yet the People of the Lie "are characterized by their absolute refusal to tolerate a sense of their own sinfulness."[12] Unwilling to acknowledge their sin, they are robbed of grace. Lacking the capacity to be wrong, they cannot make relationships right. Such people take life from others. They kill in spirit, if not in body. The People of the Lie are a rapidly spreading cancer that must be removed before vital organs are eaten away. They must be removed from the community to save the community. Anyone in church leadership knows the rare and deadly person I am speaking of.

Even in the rare instance when a Dave is asked to leave the community to save the community, the ultimate goal is to save Dave's soul, too. Paul does not merely tell the Corinthian church to turn the guilty person over to Satan. He instructs them to take such harsh measures "so that the sinful nature may be destroyed and his spirit saved on the day of the Lord."[13] Grace and redemption are the goals of even the harshest forms of love.

Counselors call this drastic step of removing a dangerous person from the community an "intervention." The abusive family member is confronted with his behaviors by the whole family and is told to get help or remove him- or herself from the family. Often the person being confronted is so self-deceived that it takes an encounter with the entire family to pierce the veil of lies he or she is hiding behind. Still, interventions often fail. The abusive family member, unable to bear the light, blames the family and storms off in rage.

But not always.

The hard, firm, tear-stained words of a caring family choosing to no longer enable a loved one's self-destruction can be the kindest words of all. Church discipline is simply the intervention process being carried out within the spiritual family.

The hard/kind words of an intervention may save the community and may also save the soul of the person hearing the words. That's why we must speak them.

BLACK ELK STILL SPEAKS

Shortly before the end of the twentieth century, HarperCollins publishers surveyed scholars and editors for their votes on the top one hundred spiritual and religious books of the century. The number-one book on the list was *Black Elk Speaks*. Black Elk was an Oglala Sioux holy man who grew up on the windswept hills of South Dakota when buffalo was still the staple diet of the Plains tribes. He took coins from the pockets of Custer's dead soldiers after their defeat at Little Big Horn. Later, he witnessed the slaughter of American Indians at Wounded Knee, the end of the Indian way of life, and the beginning of life on the reservation.

Black Elk was a highly spiritual man. He worshiped a Father God whom he called Great Spirit, but he also practiced healing by calling upon the spirits of animals he shared the earth with.

The environmental movement was gaining momentum in the 1960s and 1970s. Young people especially were seeking a spirituality that reflected their love for the planet. But they didn't find an earth-affirming spirituality in the church. Native American reverence for the earth seemed a helpful corrective to the eco-abuses of a supposedly "Christian" nation that manufactured cars that got twelve miles to the gallon and imported ashtrays made from African gorilla feet. *Black Elk Speaks* became mandatory reading for anyone interested in saving the planet and thinking about that work in spiritual terms.[1]

In 1967, while thousands of young people were snatching up copies of *Black Elk Speaks* at campus bookstores, a history professor at UCLA wrote a famous essay called "The Historical Roots of Our Ecological Crisis." Lynne White's essay appeared in *Science* magazine and was widely read by the same young people who were reading *Black Elk Speaks*. Professor White blamed the church for the world's ecological crisis: "Christianity is the most anthropocentric religion the world has seen," he wrote. "[It] not only established a dualism of man and nature but also insisted that it is God's will that man exploit nature for his proper ends."[2] Christian theology, White argued, has led Western civilization to rape the planet.

Sadly, White had a valid point. I was in seminary when James Watt, Secretary of the Interior under Ronald Reagan and an outspoken Christian, declared, "We don't have to protect the environment. The Second Coming is at hand."[3] What surprises me now is that his comments didn't surprise me back then. I spent seven years in seminary, but I didn't hear even one lecture on the church's responsibility to protect the planet. I did, however, spend hundreds of hours poring over confusing texts from Revelation and the book of Daniel that allegedly foretold how the world would end. Steeped in a particular brand of end-times theory, or "eschatology," that emphasized a fiery end to the world on the day of Armageddon, it seemed like a waste of time to care for the environment. Besides, souls are what matter. Why worry about a cursed earth that is doomed to burn up anyway? It's no surprise that environmentally sensitive people did not flock to the churches that seminarians such as I went out to start and lead. They turned to *Black Elk Speaks* instead.

A few years ago, however, it began to dawn on me that the church's mission included caring for and serving the earth. Brian McLaren's book *A New Kind of Christian* had just arrived from Amazon.com. Dan Poole, the struggling pastor who is the book's primary narrator, describes sitting on the speaker's platform at a Christian education conference alongside several prominent speakers. One of the speakers was asked what he thought about the way people are blending Christian symbols with symbols from earth religions. The speaker said it was a sure sign that the West was plummeting into moral darkness. Pastor Dan replied that he saw it differently. Perhaps our neighbors' interest in earth spirituality is an *opportunity* for the church, he said, rather than a threat. The church does and should care about the planet. When we recover the lost discipline of creation stewardship, we may have a fuller gospel to share with people who hang both crosses and dream catchers from the rearview mirrors in their cars.[4]

After reading *A New Kind of Christian,* I spoke on Palm Sunday about the three reconciling works of the cross. I began by reminding the people that God is reconciling human beings to himself through the cross. This was familiar ground.

My second point was that God is reconciling human beings to one another through the cross. This was still fairly familiar ground, and though I didn't get an amen, I didn't get any frowns.

I ended the sermon by urging the people to consider a biblical truth we hadn't looked at before: "The third effect of the cross," I began, "was to restore our relationship with the earth." I paused. We were definitely not on familiar ground now. "God is, through the cross, restoring the earth to what it was intended to be like." Then I read from the eighth chapter of Paul's letter to the Romans where he is working out the implications of the cross on all of life: "The creation itself will be liberated from its bondage to decay and brought into the glorious freedom of the children of God."[5] God is in the process of liberating not just souls but the entire planet from its bondage to sin.

Realizing I might be raising suspicions that I was "going green," I took the congregation to several texts in the Old Testament and said that "a surprising number of God's laws teach the people how to live in harmony with the land, not to worship the land like everybody else did, but to serve the land and care for the land and not rape the land."[6]

"People of the cross care about the earth," I went on. "There is a Christian approach to creation stewardship we ought to think about and express."

Unsure of how far onto thin ice I had skated, I decided to go ahead and put all my cards on the table. I closed the Palm Sunday sermon with these words:

> I wonder what would happen if we became known as a community that in a biblical, God-honoring way cared for the earth.... Why are people going to the New Age, to Eastern spirituality, to Indian spirituality? I think it is because we haven't had anything to say to people who care about the earth. And so the only thing they know to do is worship it. I wonder what would happen if we recaptured a Christian vision for the stewardship of the earth?

I shouldn't have worried. Our people have a nose for truth, even when it's truth they haven't thought about before. Within days, Rac Cox, a manager with Oak Ridge National Labs; Bill Park, a professor in agricultural economics at the University of Tennessee; Ginny Routhe, an elementary school teacher; and Lyndsay Moseley and Aaron Routhe, both graduate students at the University of Tennessee, had submitted a proposal to our elders to teach a twelve-week class on The Biblical Basis for Creation Stewardship. I took the class when I wasn't preaching and read the class bibliography and notes when I was.

I brought four questions with me into that classroom.

I was troubled by the seemingly oppressive wording of Genesis 1:28 where God ordered Adam and Eve to "fill the earth and subdue it. Rule over the fish of the sea and the birds of the air and over every living creature that moves on the ground." Words like *subdue* and *rule* are the very ones Professor White was thinking of when he wrote his article laying the ecological crisis at the feet of the church. Isn't this text a mandate for domination and exploitation?

Our teachers reminded us that scripture must always be read in light of other scriptures on the same subject. Genesis 2:15 has God telling man to "work and take care of" the garden. These words can easily be translated "serve and protect." Other texts warn the Hebrews against polluting or defiling the land and even command that they let the land rest. God's people, the church, are to exercise caring management of the land.

A second question bothered me. People writing about the environment and spirituality often blend God and earth together. The earth becomes God, and we worship the earth. "Love your Mother" urges the bumper sticker. Yet the opening pages of the bible introduce us to a God who *created* the universe. Can a Christian love the earth without worshiping it?

I found the answer in some of the class's homework assignments. The God of the bible is both transcendent (far away) and immanent (very close). Christianity for the past several centuries has stressed God's transcendence. Yet God is also immanent, involved in the world he created. God both creates and sustains the earth. As Psalm 104 says,

These all look to you
    to give them their food at the proper time.
When you give it to them,
    they gather it up;
when you open your hand,
    they are satisfied with good things.
When you hide your face,
    they are terrified;
when you take away their breath,
    they die and return to the dust.

When you send your Spirit,
  they are created,
  and you renew the face of the earth.[7]

God is involved with the world he created. Rereading some articles months later, I realized that I had been clinging to a transcendent God without fully appreciating his immanence. I also realized that Black Elk and I have more in common than I first thought: We both sense that God is mysteriously present in nature.

The third question I lugged with me into the creation stewardship class came from a brief encounter with a famous poem of Saint Francis called "The Canticle of Brother Sun" in which the great saint refers to "Brother Sun and Sister Moon."

I had always been troubled by language identifying human beings too closely with the earth, the planets, and the earth's creatures, because of texts such as Genesis 1:27 that teach that human beings are made in the image of God. No text teaches that the sun or the wind or the moon is made in God's image. Can it be right to speak of Brother Sun and Sister Moon? Am I not in danger of winding up with the neopantheism of a Disney movie?

My instructors directed me to a book written by the late evangelical theologian Francis Schaeffer titled *Pollution and the Death of Man: The Christian View of Ecology*. Schaeffer explains that "man is separated from nature because he is made in the image of God…but he is united to all other creatures as being created."[8] Human beings are special because we are made in God's image. But we are also interwoven into the web of life, related to and dependent upon every other living member of the ecosystem.

The final theological puzzle piece that I carried into the class is the one voiced by James Watt. The bible does say that the world will end in fire, so isn't working for the good of a doomed planet like shuffling deck chairs on the *Titanic*? The apostle Peter wrote that "the day of the Lord will come like a thief. The heavens will disappear with a roar; the elements will be destroyed by fire, and the earth and everything in it will be laid bare."⁹

The word for *fire,* the class's teachers pointed out, is the Greek word that we get our word *cauterize* from. It can mean "to purify." They also pointed out that the Greek word for *laid bare* means "to be discovered." One possible way to read 2 Peter 3:10 is that the world will be purified at the end of the age and transformed into a new earth. Out of the fires of Armageddon, a new earth will be discovered.

This understanding did seem to fit better with the many hopeful statements the bible makes about the world's future, promising that the earth will one day be "liberated from its bondage," that it will become "a new heaven and a new earth," and that the earth will one day be a place where "there will be no more death or mourning or crying or pain, for the old order of things has passed away."¹⁰

I am convinced that the church must understand caring for the earth as a vital part of its mission. We must be like William Wilberforce, the Christian social reformer who brought about the abolition of slavery in the British Empire and worked for fifty years to protect children by the passing of child-labor laws. He also was involved in the founding of the Royal Society for the Prevention of Cruelty to Animals.

And here's a little-known fact about Black Elk: He became a Christian after he gave the interviews that resulted in *Black Elk Speaks.* The man who spoke such eloquent words of Native American spirituality spent the last thirty years of his life speaking about Jesus to his own people on the Pine Ridge Reservation. In the final years of his life, he traveled to the Arapahos, the Winnebagoes, and the Omahas to talk about his relationship with Jesus.

The account of Black Elk's conversion is sketchy. He apparently converted after a dramatic encounter at the bedside of a dying child. He had been serving the family as a medicine man and pleading with the spirits to heal the child. A priest the villagers named Ate Ptecala, or "little Father," prayed for the dying child and asked the medicine man to stop conjuring spirits. Black Elk never practiced medicine again after that and joined the Catholic Church two weeks later. The medicine man had found the church.

Shortly before his death, he wrote, "I am a Christian.... Thirty years ago I was a real Indian and knew a little about the Great Spirit—the Wakantanka. I was a good dancer.... I was a good Indian; but now I am better."[11] Black Elk first met God in the wind and the sun and the rain of the South Dakota plains. He came to know God more fully through the church. He did not compromise his identity as a creation-loving Indian by converting to Christianity. He became a better one.

THE CHURCH AND OTHER RELIGIONS

At eleven o'clock in the morning on the Friday after the terrorist attacks of September 11, the nation gathered via television in Washington's National Cathedral for a prayer service. After the seating of the president and other officials, the clergy presiding over the service walked the aisle of the cathedral and took their seats on the platform. They were evangelist Billy Graham, African American Methodist pastor Kirbyjon Caldwell, Episcopal bishop Jane Dixon, Catholic cardinal Theodore McCarrick, Muslim imam Muzammil Siddiqi, and Rabbi Joshua Haberman. After the elderly Reverend Graham was escorted to his seat, Reverend Dixon took the podium. Her words set the tone for the morning: "Those of us who are gathered here—Muslim, Jew, Christian, Sikh, Buddhist, Hindu—all people of faith want to say to this nation and to the world that love is stronger than hate."[1]

If America ever was a Christian nation in the past, we are not one today. Most Americans believe in God but choose to relate to him through an ever-expanding diversity of religious expressions. Wellesley College, for example, has more than twenty-one religions represented on a campus of only 2,300 students. MIT sponsors twenty-eight student religious organizations, ranging from the Chinese Bible Fellowship to the Zoroastrian Association. Fly into Toledo's Express Airport and cut south on Interstate 75 through Ohio's rolling farmland, and you'll soon see a towering white dome. The beautiful building is a mosque, spiritual home to the thousands of Muslims who have moved to northern Ohio.

Islam is the fastest-growing religion in America, numbering 5.5 million adherents. On June 26, 1991, Imam Siraj Wahhaj of Brooklyn opened a session of the U.S. House of Representatives with prayer. Six months later, Imam W. Deen Mohammed opened a session of the U.S. Senate by praying to Allah.[2] In April 1990, the city council of Savannah, Georgia, issued a proclamation recognizing Islam as "a vital part of the United States of America and of the city of Savannah," acknowledging that "many of the African slaves brought to our country were followers of the religion of Al-Islam."[3] The mayor and the city council also asked that "the religion of Al-Islam be given equal acknowledgment and recognition as other religious bodies in our great city."[4] British prime minister Tony Blair, while not a Muslim, has read the Koran three times.[5]

We are not in a steepled Protestant church in Kansas anymore, Toto. Religious pluralism is here to stay, which raises an interesting question: How should the church relate to other faith communities?

One prominent evangelist drew fire shortly after the September 11 terrorist attacks when he told an interviewer he thought Islam was "a very evil and wicked religion."[6] Another prominent evangelical leader followed suit when he called the prophet Mohammed a "demon-possessed pedophile."[7] When the University of North Carolina required incoming freshmen to read *Approaching the Qur'an,* the university was sued by the Family Policy Network. A North Carolina legislator lent his support to the lawsuit, saying, "I don't want the students in the university system required to study this evil."[8]

Many churches offer this response to the idea of religious pluralism: Other religions are evil, even demon possessed; there is nothing good about them. I once held this view, basing my belief on texts such as 1 Timothy 4:1, which warns that "some will abandon the faith and follow deceiving spirits and things taught by demons." Religion can become demonic, evil, and utterly destructive. How else can we explain the child sacrifices offered to the Canaanite god Molech? How else can we explain the altars of the Aztecs, still soaked with the stains of human blood? How else can we describe the religious caste system in India that justifies oppression and discrimination? For that matter, how else can we explain the bloody Islamic jihads that have taken place in many parts of the world over the centuries or the Crusades that were carried out by church-sanctioned soldiers from Europe who waged war against various infidels? Religion can and does become evil.

But does that mean that everything about a religion is evil? My mind began to change one sweltering October evening in the southern coastal city of Nha Trang, Vietnam. Orphans roam the streets of Vietnam's largest cities, selling postcards, candy, and, in the saddest cases, their bodies. This particular evening our team was visiting a Buddhist temple with an enormous statue of the Buddha that overlooks Nha Trang's harbor. We got lost on the way and arrived at the temple near dusk. Dozens of orphans swarmed our van begging for money so they could attend a fenced-in school barely visible next to the temple. One of the children spoke English. She explained that the orphans sleep in the temple. The monks keep the orphans alive by feeding them bowls of rice. Vietnam's orphans are often cared for by Buddhist monks. Buddhists, Hindus, Muslims, and Jews work for justice and fill rice bowls in the darkest, dirtiest corners of our planet. Surely this is not evil.

I once believed I had nothing to learn from other religions. But my spiritual arrogance began to wilt as I listened to William L. Shirer's *Gandhi* on tape while commuting to work one summer. The Hindu leader Mohandas Gandhi led a fifth of humanity to independence in the 1940s. Rising each day at 2 a.m. to read either the Hindu or the Christian scriptures and say prayers, he somehow managed to live the life of a holy man while leading a revolution. India in the 1940s was not unlike the Jim Crow American South. The British Empire ruled India's 500 million citizens with an iron fist, humiliating them with discriminatory laws and abusive police tactics.

Gandhi trained in London as a lawyer and then moved to South Africa where he was beaten and imprisoned for his outspoken resistance to the racist government there. (He began working for civil rights in South Africa after being thrown out of a first-class train car because of the color of his skin.) Returning to India and being confronted with the injustice of the British domination of his people, Gandhi began to pray and think. He knew India's citizens were no match for the mighty British military, though even if they had been, the Hindu leader would no doubt have sought a nonviolent way to fight back. His decision was to call for a one-day work stoppage. Shops closed. Traffic ceased. The country shut down for a day. Today the resistance technique of nonviolent civil disobedience is practiced around the world. Gandhi was the first to try it.

One of his most memorable peaceful acts of defiance was the famous 240-mile Salt March. The British had a monopoly over the salt trade in India. Indian citizens produced the salt, and the British took the profits. Gandhi began walking toward the sea. Along the way, a million peasants joined the march. When he arrived at the coast, Gandhi waded into the small pools that collect ocean salt, scooped up a handful, and held it into the air, a gesture of defiance to the Empire. Britain could mine its own salt from now on.

Britain fought back. Police waded into peaceful demonstrations and beat protestors to the ground. Gandhi, influenced both by the teachings of Hinduism and by Jesus's instruction to turn the other cheek when struck by an enemy, taught his followers to step up and receive a beating as soon as the man or woman in front of them fell. Authorities hauled Gandhi into court. He asked for the maximum sentence. In the end he spent more than six years in British jails.

In the final years of his life, Gandhi chose to combat his oppressor with the weapon of fasting. He pledged to fast until death unless his demands were met. Unbelievably, the tactic worked. The man Indians had come to lovingly call the Great Soul was summoned to London to meet with the king. Prime Minister Winston Churchill grumbled at "the nauseating and humiliating spectacle of this one-time Inner Temple lawyer, now seditious fakir, striding half-naked on the steps of the Viceroy's palace, there to negotiate and parley on equal terms with the representative of the King Emperor."[9] India was granted independence in 1948, the year of Gandhi's death.

The Great Soul also took on the injustices his own people brought upon themselves through the caste system rooted in the Hindu doctrine of karma. The caste system ranks human beings on a ladder of status. There are about five thousand rungs on the caste ladder. It is seen as sinful to try to improve your rank. The lowest caste, the Untouchables, live in filthy slums and sweep streets and clean toilets, tasks Hindus from loftier castes never touch. If confronted by another Hindu, an Untouchable cringes and slinks away.

Gandhi, at the risk of losing popularity among his Hindu countrymen, gave the Untouchables a new name: the *Harijans,* the Children of God. He called the Untouchables his brothers and sisters and stayed in their homes whenever he could, sometimes even cleaning their toilets. When Lord Mountbatten was being considered for the honorary post of Governor General in post-independence India, Gandhi proposed an alternate candidate: an Untouchable street sweeper "of stout heart, incorruptible and crystal-like in her purity."[10] Gandhi's candidate didn't win, but his campaign to expose the darkness of the caste system ultimately led to new laws across India that toned down the system's severest injustices.[11]

Christians have significant differences with Hindus on matters of great importance. Yet Christians have much to learn from Hindus like Mohandas Gandhi. (Once asked what he thought about Western civilization, Gandhi replied, "I think it would be a great idea.")

Martin Luther King, Jr., entered Crozer Theological Seminary in Chester, Pennsylvania, in September 1948 and immediately began what he calls in his autobiography "a serious intellectual quest for a method to eliminate social evil."[12] One Sunday afternoon in 1949, that quest took him to Philadelphia to hear Dr. Mordecai Johnson, president of Howard University, preach for the Fellowship House of Pennsylvania. Here is how Dr. King remembers the event:

> Dr. Johnson had just returned from a trip to India, and, to my great interest, he spoke of the life and teachings of Mahatma Gandhi. His message was so profound and electrifying that I left the meeting and bought a half-dozen books on Gandhi's life and works.... It was in this Gandhian emphasis on love and nonviolence that I discovered the method for social reform that I had been seeking.[13]

Eleven years later, shortly after the Montgomery boycott, King traveled to India to visit with Gandhi's friends and followers. "I was delighted that the Gandhians accepted us with open arms," he recalled. "They praised our experiment with the nonviolent resistance technique at Montgomery."[14] One evening Dr. King was invited to speak at a high school for the children of Untouchables. The principle introduced him as "a fellow untouchable from the United States of America." Recalling the event later in a sermon at Ebenezer Baptist Church, he admitted that he was shocked at first, but then he realized, "Yes, I am an untouchable, and every Negro in the United States of America is an untouchable."[15] The writer who influenced Martin Luther King, Jr., the most while he was studying in a Christian seminary was a Hindu.

The church's scriptures do not always portray adherents of other religions as evil. The book of Acts describes the Roman soldier Cornelius as "devout and God-fearing; he gave generously to those in need and prayed to God regularly." An angel tells this devout man, who at this point had never heard of Jesus Christ, "Your prayers and gifts to the poor have come up as a memorial offering before God."[16] The Magi who first worshiped the Christ child were astrologers from the Orient.[17] The apostle Paul, in his sermon to the philosophers of Athens, quoted one of their own poets and commended the writer for being "very religious."[18] Across the ages the church's great thinkers have respected and built upon certain teachings of other faiths and philosophies. Aquinas learned from Aristotle. Augustine's thought was sharpened by Plato's.

Impressed by the beauty and wisdom and compassion found in the great world religions, some churches have chosen to regard other faith communities as simply differing expressions of one global religion. Edmund Perry, who chaired the Department of History and Literature of Religions at Northwestern University, saw it that way. An ordained Methodist minister, Perry spent many semesters in Sri Lanka studying Buddhism under Walpola Rahula. Perry was convinced that his Christianity and Rahula's Buddhism were different expressions of the same faith. Perry and I disagreed on nearly every possible theological point. We also loved each other very much.

Sipping tea in his study, we toured the great questions that twenty-year-old religious-studies students wrestle with—sex, frat parties, Karl Barth's *Dogmatics in Outline,* Paul Tillich's *Ultimate Concern.* Frequently we talked about the book Perry was writing with a former student who had become a Buddhist scholar. The book is called *A World Theology.* I understand it has become something of a classic in the field of comparative religion, offering one of the best arguments for the belief that all religions are different expressions of the same religious reality.

I found Perry's book in the University of Tennessee library when I was collecting material for this essay. I opened the first page, waded through the academic language, and was taken back to those Sunday afternoons in Evanston, Illinois. Here's a description of the book from its introduction:

In *A World Theology*, a Christian theologian and an atheistic Buddhist philosopher examine five major world religions—Hinduism, Buddhism, Judaism, Christianity, and Islam—to demonstrate that each is a particular expression of a central spiritual reality shared by all humankind.[19]

I have often longed to spend another Sunday afternoon sipping tea with Dr. Perry. Yet I can't agree with him on this point. The sacred texts the church calls scripture make too many assertions that Christianity is the religion that most fully reveals the living God, and the church as the faith community in which that living God is best worshiped, served, and known.

Joshua challenged the people of Israel to "throw away the gods your forefathers worshiped beyond the River and in Egypt, and serve the LORD."[20] Jesus commanded the tiny community that would become the first church to "make disciples of all the nations,"[21] which means inviting people of other faith communities to enter our own. The apostle Paul, writing to the Christians in Corinth, observed that "even if there are so-called gods…, for us there is but one God, the Father, from whom all things came and for whom we live; and there is but one Lord, Jesus Christ, through whom all things came and through whom we live. But not everyone knows this."[22] I can't imagine Jesus encouraging the people he met to merely be faithful within their own religions when he said, "I am the way and the truth and the life. No one comes to the Father except through me."[23] And I can't ignore the conclusion of a sermon Peter preached in a city of a hundred faiths: "Salvation is found in no one else, for there is no other name under heaven given to men by which we must be saved."[24]

I am groping toward a faithful way for the church to relate to other religions in a part of the West that is rapidly becoming Muslim, Hindu, Buddhist, Jewish, and lots more. How can the church respect, honor, learn from, and even partner with other faith communities while humbly and vigorously celebrating the supreme beauty and matchless power and ultimate hope of Jesus Christ?

Thinking people around the world see religions retrenching behind the barbed-wire barriers of fundamentalism, sending suicide bombers into Jewish supermarkets, bulldozers into Palestinian houses, and bayonets into the chests of Bosnian Serbs. It's understandable why many wish everyone could agree that all religions are singing different verses of the same song. The concern for world peace, which lies behind this argument, is rooted in reality.

But do we all have to believe the same things in order to get along?

A more compelling (and more realistic) dream is one of a human race in which people who believe very differently learn how to respect and tolerate one another, even *because* of their differences. Would I be loving my Muslim friend Sean if I were to ignore our distinct religious differences? Or would I love him better by listening carefully to what he believes, sharing carefully what I believe, and then engaging in a lively dialogue? Wouldn't we both be better off?

Don't we consider it necessary and beneficial for political scientists and economists and historians to argue their conflicting beliefs through journals and conferences and classrooms and books? Don't we cherish our freedom to argue the president's foreign policy or tax plan, to vote for whomever we choose, to have voter forums and candidate debates and editorials in the newspaper? Hasn't the free exchange of ideas helped build a strong democracy? Why then do we fear openness and dialogue among religions? Probably because political scientists usually don't blow up those who disagree with them, while religious fundamentalists sometimes do.

Like it or not, healthy religions are passionate religions. The religious pluralism witnessed on the platform of the National Cathedral on September 14, 2001, is not going away. The real differences between America's religions are not likely to go away either. But rather than fearing religious pluralism, we can embrace it as an opportunity to practice the love of Christ in a divided world. While we hold deeply to our own beliefs and eagerly share them with others, we can nonetheless build relationships with and work alongside different faith communities.

Shortly after the September 11 attacks, Mike Boyd, a local pastor, asked me to go with him to visit Knoxville's only mosque. We arrived shortly before the noon prayer service was ending. Our guests greeted us a little reluctantly, fearing perhaps that we had come to blame them for the terrorist attacks. They invited us into a small study next to the prayer room. Mike got right to the point.

"You are our neighbors," he said. "We're proud to have you in our community. We know this is a frightening time for the Muslim community. If there is any way we can help you, let us know. And if anyone tries to hurt you, we want to know that, too."

We hugged one another, walked past a wall lined with the shoes of men still praying, and stepped outside into a hopeful September sun.

STILL POINT IN THE
TURNING WORLD

I'm writing this essay in a small, cinder-block guestroom of the Abbey of Gethsemani, a Trappist monastery lost in rolling blue-green hills about fifty miles and a thousand years away from Lexington, Kentucky. Directions downloaded from *www.monks.org* instructed me to turn left at the Kwik Mart in Culver and look for the blinking stoplight three miles down Highway 247, a rural road that winds past horse farms and naive cattle grazing near a white barn bearing the sign "Beef: It's What's for Dinner." The monastery appeared suddenly on the left, looking not unlike the campus of a small college fortunate enough to own hundreds of unspoiled Kentucky woodlands. A white-brick bell tower with a simple black steeple stands watch next to the church.

The bell begins a monk's day at 3:00 a.m. and then summons the community to prayer seven times a day. The church is flanked by a guesthouse to the north and monks' quarters to the south. A brick fence painted white circles the property tentatively, less a protection than a sacred boundary.

I arrived well after the 6:30 p.m. check-in time as the sun was setting over the large cross that stands like a sentry on a hill across from the monastery. A simple graveyard of white stone crosses greeted me as I carried my bags and my laptop into the guesthouse, and I remembered a line from Thomas Merton about monks' dying with smiles on their faces.

"I'm sorry for coming so late," I apologized to the elderly monk who shuffled downstairs to unlock the door and give me my room key.

"That's all right," he said. "You are here."

I am here because I've been here before, and I've found Gethsemani a sacred place. I meet God here.

There is a sense in which every place can be a sacred place because God is in every place. And there is a danger in focusing too much on sacred places as if God were bound too tightly to the limits of time and space. The Old Testament does link God's presence in a unique way with the temple, but on this side of the cross, *we* are the temple where God dwells, built out of the living stones of our lives.[1] Those who follow Christ have become God's dwelling place on earth. God is equally at home with us in a catacomb or jungle hut as he is in a Gothic cathedral.

The church is people, not a building. We *can* meet God anywhere. Yet many of us who have protested the loudest that "the church is not a building" are humbly discovering that church buildings can indeed be sacred places that enhance our encounters with God.

Reflecting on a semester he spent teaching at the North American College in Rome, Henri Nouwen wrote, "The churches of Rome are like beautiful frames around empty spaces witnessing to him who is the quiet, still center of human life." In the middle of a bustling city, "there are the domes of Rome pointing to the places set apart for the Holy One."[2]

But isn't all of life set apart for the Holy One?

"Whatever you do," Paul wrote, "whether in word or deed, do it all in the name of the Lord Jesus."[3] Every place we go in the rhythms of our daily lives ought to be set apart for the Holy One. Our office cubicle ought to be set apart to God. The kitchen in which we prepare meals ought to be set apart to God. The shop where we repair cars for a living ought to be set apart to God. All of life is sacred and offers an opportunity to worship God.

The problem with kitchens and cubicles and repair shops is that not much in them reminds us of God. Kitchens and cubicles and shops don't invite us to look up. Churches, especially churches that grasp the spiritual power of space, shape, symbol, form, and beauty, do issue such an invitation.

After twenty years of working in the suburbs, I recently moved into a downtown office. Our city, on its better days, is a carnival of passions and life. Abandoned warehouses are being transformed into trendy townhouses. Restaurants are opening in buildings once boarded up. Rockabilly bands draw hundreds into the streets on hot summer nights to dance and eat bratwurst. Bankers and lawyers in navy suits and red ties hurry by, closing deals on their cell phones. Backpack-laden college students rush to class. Sweatsuit-clad city dwellers pour into the YMCA to swim a few laps or play basketball. Reporters rush from the City County Building to file their stories before deadline. Tourists stream into our new convention center. I like working in our city.

I also find life in the city impersonal and spiritually disorienting. A quick glance out my window scans several billboards, a tired Holiday Inn, several sterile office towers that look like the Communists designed them, a fire station, and endless traffic. Sirens pierce the air several times an hour. Homeless men and women sleep under newspapers on park benches stained with pigeon droppings—mere ghosts to those who walk past them. Behind my office building forgotten railway cars rot on tracks that lead nowhere. Broken liquor bottles sparkle like fool's gold beneath clumps of gangly bushes. Sometimes on February nights when I am walking to my Pontiac after work and a bitter rain sweeps down from the Cumberland Plateau, I feel alone and afraid and abandoned by God.

Searching for new routes to my office one morning, I drove by St.

John's Cathedral, a stately Episcopal church that has graced the center of our city for more than one hundred years. "Morning Prayer: 8 a.m.," announced a sign on the side of the cathedral. Then beneath that line was another: "Eucharist: Wednesdays, 7 a.m."

I try to pray at St. John's once a week now. The Episcopal prayer service increases in meaning as I learn my way around the *Book of Common Prayer*. I find a deepening appreciation for the sacrament of the Eucharist. What nurtures me the most, though, is the sacrament of the place itself.

A sacrament, as I understand it, is something physical that helps a person encounter God. God knows we are earthbound people. He gives us the bread and the cup, baptism, and even his own Son wrapped up in human flesh as sacraments, physically real things that connect us with God's heart and remind us of what is real but unseen. A place can be sacramental, too, when the space is crafted with an eye toward heaven. The chapel in St. John's Cathedral has become a sacrament for me, a beautiful frame "around empty spaces witnessing to him who is the quiet, still center of all human life."

Stained-glass windows paint the gospel story in deep purples and regal reds, the story told differently each day by the shifting angles of sunlight. Dark oak pews invite me to sit but not to be entertained. A cushion on the floor invites me to kneel before the King of the universe. A flickering candle illuminating the shadows is an image of the One who is the Light of a shadowy world.

The poet T. S. Eliot described places like St. John's Cathedral as the "still point in the turning world."[4] We need these still points to remind us of what we believe: that all of life is sacred and that God is present even amidst the broken shards of a whiskey bottle. This is hard to remember sometimes. Especially in February.

THE FOUR WALLS
OF MY FREEDOM

When I enrolled in seminary in 1983, I signed a covenant in which my wife, Sandi, and I agreed to refrain from certain activities. Dancing was on the list. I signed the covenant and tore out part of my wife's soul.

Sandi loves to dance. She took every dance course that Cal State Fullerton had to offer—jazz, tap, ballet—and taught dance classes her senior year. Once, on a rare moment when she shared the dance studio with no one else, she envisioned Jesus sitting on the seats outside the studio watching her dance and smiling at the beauty of her art. This vision, I have since learned, is one of the most sacred moments in her life.

Jesus may have smiled, but most of his followers who knew Sandi during college were frowning. Christian friends warned her that being part of "the dance world" might stain her moral purity. And besides, wouldn't a serious Christian devote those hours to more worthy pursuits such as bible study, prayer, and evangelism?

That day in 1983 when I asked Sandi to sign a covenant in which she promised not to dance, I was inflicting more damage than her college friends' comments ever did. In a way, I was telling her that godly people don't dance. I was telling her that the creative passions of her heart are impure. I was telling her that Jesus hadn't been smiling on her dancing.

I was wrong.

Today we are part of a spiritual community that encourages the arts as a valid expression of worship. Sandi has been dancing again for several years now. She takes a class here and there and does the choreography for a musical-theater class at a local high school. But we both know that the best years of her dancing are lost forever. We grieve.

I have a close friend who has built an impressive business from scratch. He has an astounding nose for new opportunities, a remarkable knack for closing deals, and a God-given capacity for making money. More important, he is a caring and wise father. Knowing the risks of the rough-and-tumble business world, he has done everything a man can do to prepare his sons to survive in the real world. He has taken his boys on business trips and brought them into high-level staff meetings. He has given his boys everything they need to make their way in the business world.

His oldest son, a devout Christian with numerous talents, is graduating from college. He wants to write songs.

Dad is crushed because he doesn't want his son waiting tables in a seedy Nashville bar when he's thirty-five. He's also crushed, I think, because songwriting as a vocation doesn't rank very high in his bottom-line world. To his credit, my friend is encouraging his son to follow his dreams while gently reminding him (or asking me to remind him) of the nasty fiscal realities of life (e.g., Dad won't foot the bill forever).

Once, while teaching English at a Christian college, I asked a class of freshmen to write a paper on C. S. Lewis's *The Lion, the Witch and the Wardrobe*. One student refused: Didn't I know there were talking animals and magic and witches in that book? Lewis was likely not even a Christian, she informed me. Fantasy, she argued, is the stuff of paganism.

The church, at least the part of the church I am most familiar with, has not blessed its artists. We've patted them on the head and encouraged them to start doing more practical things. Even worse, at times we've forbidden them from practicing their art at all. Christian suspicion about art is rooted in the Reformation. Zwingli and Calvin banned all paintings and sculpture in the church because they believed this kind of art violated the second commandment: "You shall not make for yourself an idol."[1]

Yet God himself ordered his people to fill his house with beautiful art not long after he had given them the Ten Commandments. Angels were woven into tent curtains and into the veil that hung in the entrance to the Holy of Holies. Statues of cherubim were sculpted. Almond flowers with buds and blossoms were carved into the cups of the lampstand. Blue pomegranates were woven around the hems of the priestly garments.[2] God even selected certain artists to oversee the creative process:

> Then the LORD said to Moses, "See, I have chosen Bezalel son of Uri, the son of Hur, of the tribe of Judah, and I have filled him with the Spirit of God, with skill, ability and knowledge in all kinds of crafts—to make artistic designs for work in gold, silver and bronze, to cut and set stones, to work in wood, and to engage in all kinds of craftsmanship.... Also I have given skill to all the craftsmen to make everything I have commanded you."[3]

The church, the new tabernacle of God, ought to be equally filled with art and artists—an incubator for creativity. Sadly, the artist must often step outside the church to pursue his or her work.

Vincent van Gogh began his professional life as a pastor to Dutch coal workers. But mind-numbing poverty and humiliating encounters with the religious leadership drove him away from the faith. And then *Crows over a Cornfield* and *Starry Night* and *Self-Portrait* came from his brush. Some of his best paintings came from his days in an insane asylum shortly before he committed suicide. He died miserable, alone, insane. Why did the church lose van Gogh?

The pioneering psychologist Carl Jung believed great art could never come from within the church because of closed systems of religion. This has no doubt been the case, but does it have to be?

The God who confronts us in the opening page of the bible is an artist. Five times in the opening verses of Genesis we read, "So God created." One of those times we also read "So God created man in his own image."[4] God creates. We are most like him when we create. The church is a community of the creative.

So where are the poets? Where are the dancers? Where are the sculptors? Where are the writers? Where are the composers? Where are the producers? Aren't we getting tired of trotting out the names of long-dead British guys when someone asks for an outstanding artist who works within the church? The wind has shifted, if only slightly. Fresh breezes appear to be kicking up. The church is beginning to bless her artists. We are rediscovering that creating beauty is a core work of the church.

Knoxville, Tennessee, is a far cry from Broadway, but there are encouraging signs even in our corner of the world. The Bijou, our local musical-theater company, held auditions for the cast of *Annie*. More than a dozen Christians won important roles. Significantly, they did so with the blessing of their churches. Chad, a talented youth minister, recently left student ministry to pursue a lifelong dream of making films. The New City Café, a downtown ministry arm of Knoxville's churches, holds regular poetry-reading nights and artist workshops. The Ballet Gloria dance troupe provides the church's dancers a forum to practice their art.

But most Christians still must practice their art outside the church. I grudgingly find Jung's critique uncomfortably near the mark in my own creative work as a writer. Trained to work and think and dream within the boundaries of faith, I fear mystery like a dangling participle and strain to offer detailed answers when simply raising questions gets closer to the truth of God. I began to write a bad novel once. An editor with whom I was under contract to write another book kindly read the first drafts. "Let's stick with nonfiction for now," his e-mail said. The novel lacked wildness. The characters' mouths were stuffed with minisermonettes, the dialogue was staged, and the plot was predictable. I wrote it with a thousand editors reading over my shoulder—pastors from years past and seminary professors and my wife's college friends all hovered around me as I typed. I can't blame my failure as a novelist on the church, yet the fear of swerving off the well-marked highway of conservative Protestant cultural orthodoxy can often stifle creativity.

When an artist's creative impulse begins to give birth, "we are led into places we do not expect," observes author Madeleine L'Engle. It is then that we are drawn "into adventures we do not always understand."[5] We are not talking about a precise, quantifiable discipline such as accounting. We are talking about giving birth to a poem or play or pastel painting that kicks and screams and wriggles out of your hands and even learns to walk on its own. As every parent knows, children go places they are not supposed to—and so does good art.

I want to try creative writing again, but not a novel this time. I want to write a spiritual memoir. Yet I hesitate. What if the book takes wing and flies me too close to the sun? I do not find many voices within the church who even recognize this thing that I fear. I find even fewer who encourage me to face it.

These complaints, however, can be little more than sophisticated excuses. The truth is that great art has, does, and will come from within the church. This essay, like the one before it, was written at the Abbey of Gethsemani. Thomas Merton wrote *The Seven Storey Mountain* here in 1947.

That book, read by nearly a million people the first year it came out, has become a classic of twentieth-century literature; Merton has become one of the century's great poets and writers. He wrote nearly all of his books as a monk in the pre-Vatican II Roman Catholic Church under the careful eye of an abbot who read every word he wrote and sometimes forbid him from writing more than an hour a day. When he became a monk, Merton surrendered the right to leave, the right to marry, the right to take a vacation, the right to publish what he wanted, the right to earn so much as a dollar from his best-selling books. As is customary for every monk upon entering the community, he even surrendered his name. There is no Thomas Merton in the monastery graveyard. "F. Louis Merton. Died Dec. 10, 1968," reads the bronze plaque on the white cross marking his grave.

If Jung is correct, few places on earth are more likely to suffocate the creative impulse than a Trappist monastery. Here the walls are not just psychological ones. You see them every time you look out the window. Merton, however, found just the opposite to be true, calling his monastic home "the four walls of my new freedom."[6] Seventy books flowed from his pen here, as did dozens of poems, and near the end of his life, brilliant photographs. Time in a monastery is tightly woven around "the hours," seven blocks of daily prayer when the community ceases all other work. Merton reflected on how the medieval, monastic sense of time affected his writing:

> I brought all the instincts of a writer with me into the monastery, and I knew that I was bringing them, too. It was not a case of smuggling them in. And Father Master not only approved but encouraged me when I wanted to write poems and reflections and other things that came into my head in the novitiate.
>
> Already in the Christmas season I had half filled an old notebook that belonged to my Columbia days, with the ideas that came swimming into my head all through those wonderful feasts, when I was a postulant.
>
> In fact, I found that the interval after the night office, in the great silence, between four and five-thirty on the mornings of feast days was a wonderful time to write verse. After two or three hours of prayer your mind is saturated in peace and the richness

of the liturgy. The dawn is breaking outside cold windows. If it is warm, the birds are already beginning to sing. Whole blocks of imagery seem to crystallize out as it were naturally in the silence and the peace, and the lines almost write themselves.[7]

Merton found life, not death, within the walls that wove among the wooded hills outside the monastery. The ancient rhythms of this community's life together drew him ever closer toward the flame of God's love, the source of his genius. In the end he was drawn into places he didn't expect. His art, like his life, was an adventure he didn't quite understand.

Tomorrow morning the great bell in the chapel tower will sound at 3:00 a.m. I will join the monks for Vigils, clean my room, and then leave this peaceful place, having tasted a freedom found within the four walls of my faith.

ONE CHURCH, MANY CONGREGATIONS

I n a town where everyone was either Lutheran or Catholic, we were neither one." So begins the chapter titled "Protestant" in Garrison Keillor's *Lake Wobegon Days*.

Keillor continues:

We were "exclusive" Brethren, a branch that believed in keeping itself pure of false doctrine by avoiding association with the impure. Some Brethren assemblies, mostly in larger cities, were not so strict and broke bread with strangers—we referred to them as "the so-called Open Brethren," the "so-called" implying the shakiness of their position—whereas we made sure that any who fellowshipped with us were straight on all the details of the Faith, as set forth by the first Brethren who left the Anglican Church in 1865 to worship on the basis of correct principles....

Unfortunately, once free of the worldly Anglicans, these fire-brands were not content to worship in peace but turned their guns on each other. Scholarly to the core and perfect literalists every one, they set to arguing over points that, to an outsider, would have seemed very minor indeed but which to them were crucial to the Faith, including the question: if Believer A is associ-

ated with Believer B who has somehow associated himself with C
who holds a False Doctrine, must A break off association with B,
even though B does not hold the Doctrine, to avoid the taint?
The correct answer is: Yes.…

Once having tasted the pleasure of being Correct and defend-
ing True Doctrine, they kept right on and broke up at every
opportunity, until, by the time I came along, there were dozens
of tiny Brethren groups, none of which were speaking to any of
the others. [1]

The problem of disunity in the church did not begin in Lake Wobegon, Minnesota. Jesus was committed to unity but was also aware that
disunity would threaten his followers. Reclining on a cushion at a low
table covered with the leftovers of a final Passover meal, Jesus looked into
the candlelit faces of his community, looked through them into the
future—at the church to be born from their blood and words—and
prayed that his church become one. [2]

The church *did* exist as one unified family for its first three hundred
years. Brutal persecution broke out toward the end of the third century,
and many Christians renounced their faith. When the fires of persecution subsided, many of these same Christians wanted to return to the
church. A priest named Donatus argued against letting them return. The
rest of the Catholic Church disagreed. Donatus left in a huff and formed
the first breakaway denomination, the Donatists.

A hundred and fifty years later, churches in Egypt and Syria disagreed over the way the Council of Chalcedon described the mystery of
Christ as being both God and man, and they broke away. In AD 1054
the Eastern Orthodox churches broke away from the Roman Catholic
Church, disagreeing over technical wording in the Nicene Creed describing the Spirit's relationship to the Father and the Son.

The next great church split came in AD 1521 when Martin Luther was excommunicated from the Roman Catholic Church after refusing to recant his criticisms of church teaching. History has called those who followed Luther "Protestants" because they joined him in protesting abuses in the Roman Church. The Protestants, to borrow a phrase from Garrison Keillor, soon turned their guns on each other and broke apart their fellowships with bewildering speed over doctrinal matters that today seem as obscure as the ones fought over by the Lake Wobegon Brethren.

The dismembering of the body of Christ into thousands of separate pieces is a very serious matter to our Lord: He links our unity as his people with our ability to invite a neighbor into the life of God. "May they be brought to complete unity," he prayed at the Last Supper, "to let the world know that you sent me."[3] The church is a mirror reflecting the face of God to the world. A cracked mirror reflects a distorted image.

Before this chapter disintegrates into a string of platitudes, let's take a brief reality break.

Reality Check No. 1: Christians in the early church often fought like cats and dogs.

Reality Check No. 2: Nobody wants to give away the spiritual traditions and core beliefs of their spiritual family. Denominations aren't going away anytime soon.

Reality Check No. 3: Most efforts to create unity among the churches haven't succeeded.

Given these realities, what does "complete unity" look like?

The New Testament churches lived in a constant tension. On one hand, they saw themselves as members of the one church in their city— made up of all local believers. On the other hand, they identified themselves as people who worshiped at a particular person's home. Today we'd call those smaller gatherings congregations. *One church, many congregations.* That was how the early church experienced unity amidst diversity.[4]

The Greater Knoxville area has nearly seven hundred congregations. Each congregation is a valid expression of the one church of Greater

Knoxville. *One church, many congregations.* This is how today's church experiences unity amidst diversity.

Soon after the ink dried on the last New Testament letter, the new churches began selecting bishops and assigning them to oversee congregations in various cities—one bishop per city. Unity in the church flowed from the top down. The ancient world was a world of hierarchy and order. Society worked best when the channels of power were clearly marked.

Many of my Catholic friends believe this is still the way the church should work. If everyone would recognize the authority of the pope and his bishops and submit to them, the church would once again be one. But the world we live in is not as hierarchical as the ancient world. Rooted in Platonic philosophy that broke all of life into a ladder of order, the ancients had no other way to think than in a rigid, patriarchal, hierarchical fashion.

Today we understand that the nature of the universe is much more organic than it is hierarchical. The world is more like the ecosystem of a forest than a military chain of command. The "complete unity" Christ prayed for will not be found by returning to an ancient model of power and authority. Unity among our churches will emerge instead as we learn to work together as communities woven into the life web of the living body of Christ. The operative words in church unity conversations are not *power* and *authority* but *collaboration* and *partnership*.

I think I see an outline of what is emerging. Tomorrow's churches will navigate the *one church, many congregations* paradox by creating networks of churches that in turn network with one another. The one church in a city will look like a vast galaxy, with individual congregations the stars of a solar system, and many solar systems making up the galaxy. Put another way, the congregations in a city will work together like the interconnected rings of the Olympic logo, no one ring standing out from another. There will be communication but not control. There will be mutual sharing and respect and learning and cooperation with each individual congregation bringing its own special gifts to the kingdom party.

The emerging diversity within the unity of the church will be difficult to describe, hard to write about, impossible to capture on an organization chart, and frustrating to lead. We won't figure it out until long after I am dead.

But this is where we're headed.

epilogue

A few of you may be smitten by the Spirit with a yearning to pioneer a new kind of church. These final words are for you. We are living in an era of revolutionary change. Young leaders, especially, are eager to explore new territory and draw new maps. Even the bravest explorers had a vague idea of where they were heading before they left port. You should too. This book is not intended to give you answers. Instead, it's the beginning of a conversation in which you will have the last word. I've shared my ideas on the church. Now it's time to think through your own ideas.

Here's an exercise that can help you begin to envision the kind of church you and some friends may want to launch. Send an e-mail to a friend or a leader whose opinion you respect. Tell that person your dreams and hopes and fears about a new kind of church. Paint a picture of the kind of church you'd like to be a part of.

Just let it rip. Don't worry about your grammar or the internal consistency or length of your paragraphs. Tell a story if you want to. Write a poem. Natalie Goldberg, in her fun book on writing titled *Writing Down the Bones,* urges, "Sit down right now. Give me this moment. Write whatever's running through you.... Don't try to control it. Stay present with whatever comes up, and keep your hand moving."[1] That's good advice for this assignment, too.

Notes

Prologue

1. Cormac McCarthy, *Suttree* (New York: Knopf, 1992), 101-2.

Prague, 1989

1. Miroslav Václav Havel, "The Power of the Powerless," in *The Power of the Powerless: Citizens Against the State in Central Eastern Europe,* ed. John Keane (Armonk, NY: M. E. Sharpe, 1990), quoted in Václav Havel, *Václav Havel: Living in Truth,* ed. Jan Vladislav (London: Faber and Faber, 1989), 101-2.
2. John 1:5 and 1 John 1:6.
3. John 8:44. See also Revelation 20:10.
4. Genesis 12:2,3.
5. Deuteronomy 4:6 and Isaiah 42:6.
6. Matthew 5:14.
7. Exodus 19:6.
8. 1 Peter 2:9.
9. 1 Peter 2:11,12.
10. Shelly Kreykes, personal e-mail correspondence to author, September 2003. Emphasis added.
11. Julian, quoted in Stephen Neill, *A History of Christian Missions* (New York: Penguin, 1991), 37-38.
12. Stanley Hauerwas and William Willimon, *Resident Aliens: Life in the Christian Colony* (Nashville: Abingdon, 1990), 46.

The Homecoming of God

1. Ramsay MacMullen, *Paganism in the Roman Empire* (New Haven, CT: Yale University Press, 1981), 1.
2. Exodus 25:8.
3. "Then the cloud covered the Tent of Meeting, and the glory of the LORD filled the tabernacle" (Exodus 40:34).
4. Exodus 33:15-16.
5. Ezekiel 10:18.
6. See Ezekiel 37:27 and Malachi 3:1.
7. Ephesians 2:19,20-21.
8. Ephesians 2:22.
9. "The gathered church is the place of God's own personal presence, by the Spirit," writes New Testament scholar Gordon Fee. "This is what marks off God's new people from all other people on the face of the earth." (Gordon Fee, *Paul, the Spirit, and the People of God* [Peabody, MA: Hendrickson, 1996], 19.)
10. Iain Murray, *The Life of D. Martyn Lloyd-Jones: The First Forty Years,* vol. 1 (Edinburgh, Scotland: Banner of Truth Trust, 1983), 221.
11. Harvey Cox, *Fire from Heaven: Pentecostalism, Spirituality and the Reshaping of Religion in the Twenty-First Century* (New York: Addison-Wesley, 1995), 86.

Sacred Conversations

1. Mark 1:16-17.
2. Mark 3:13-14.
3. John 1:1-2. See also verses 3-14.
4. John 14:18,26.
5. John 16:13,15.
6. Matthew 28:20.
7. To read about the events following Christ's resurrection, see Acts 1–2.

Daring to Speak for God

1. Frederick Buechner, *Telling the Truth: The Gospel as Tragedy, Comedy, and Fairy Tale* (San Francisco: Harper & Row, 1977), 22-23.
2. Joshua 3:9.
3. Luke 24:27.
4. Gary Goodell, "To Preach or Not to Preach: Is That Really the Question?" July 2002, www.next-wave.org.

Prayer

1. Matthew 6:9-13.
2. Psalm 103:1-2. For more, see Benedict, *The Rule of St. Benedict,* ed. Timothy Fry (New York: Vintage, 1998).
3. Romans 8:26.
4. Hebrews 13:15.
5. Romans 15:5.

Stolen Gloves

1. Charles Spurgeon, *The Autobiography of Charles Spurgeon,* vol. 2 (Cincinnati: Curts and Jennings, 1899), 226-27.
2. The first-century, Old Testament prophet Joel, as recorded in Acts 2:18.
3. See 1 Corinthians 14:1,3,29-33.
4. Ken Gire, *Windows of the Soul: Experiencing God in New Ways* (Grand Rapids: Zondervan, 1996), 73.

Feeling God's Pleasure

1. Frederick Buechner, quoted in Ken Gire, *Windows of the Soul: Experiencing God in New Ways* (Grand Rapids: Zondervan, 1996), 71.
2. 1 Peter 4:10.
3. Parker J. Palmer, *Let Your Life Speak: Listening for the Voice of Vocation* (San Francisco: Jossey-Bass, 2000), 16.

Boundaries

1. William Manchester, *A World Lit Only by Fire: The Medieval Mind and the Renaissance* (New York: Little, Brown, 1992), 177-78.

2. See Kenneth Scott Latourette, *A History of Christianity*, vol. 1 (Peabody, MA: Hendrickson, 2003), 410.

3. Colossians 4:5; 1 Thessalonians 4:12.

4. Matthew 8:12; 18:3; 19:23-24.

5. Paul Hiebert, "The Category 'Christian' in the Mission Task," *International Review of Mission* 72 (July 1983): 421-23. The article was introduced to me in Michael A. King, *Trackless Wastes and Stars to Steer By: Christian Identity in a Homeless Age* (Scottdale, PA: Herald Press, 1990), chap. 5. This material is summarized and adapted by written permission of Paul Hiebert.

$4,285.78 per Month

1. Adapted from Ronald J. Sider, *Cup of Water, Bread of Life: Inspiring Stories About Overcoming Lopsided Christianity* (Grand Rapids: Zondervan, 1994), 33-35.

2. "Virtually every strand of biblical truth calls Christians to link word and deed in proclaiming the Good News of Christ's reign." (Ronald J. Sider, Philip N. Olson, and Heidi Rolland Unruh, *Churches That Make a Difference: Reaching Your Community with Good News and Good Works* [Grand Rapids: Baker, 2002], 46.)

3. Luke 4:18-21.

4. Matthew 9:36.

5. James 1:27.

6. Rodney Stark, *The Rise of Christianity* (Princeton, NJ: Princeton University Press, 1996), chaps. 5 and 7.

7. Stark, *The Rise of Christianity*, chaps. 5 and 7.

8. Stark, *The Rise of Christianity*, chaps. 5 and 7.

9. Stark, *The Rise of Christianity*, chaps. 5 and 7.

10. Stark, *The Rise of Christianity*, 118.

11. Matthew 25:31-46.

12. Dionysius, quoted in Adolf Harnack, *The Mission and Expansion of Christianity*, vol. 1 (New York: Putnam, 1908), 171-72.

13. Dionysius, quoted in Harnack, *The Mission and Expansion of Christianity*, 171-72.

14. Harnack, *The Mission and Expansion of Christianity*, 153-77.

15. See Agnieszka Tennant, "Counting (Helping) Hands: A Conversation with Ram Cnaan," *Books & Culture* (January/February 2003): 26.

16. Robert Wuthnow, "'I Was Thirsty'...How Congregations Serve," *Books & Culture* (January/February 2003): 24-26.

17. Wuthnow, "I Was Thirsty," 24-26.

18. Gary Simpson, quoted in Robert D. Carle and Louis A. Decaro Jr., eds., *Signs of Hope in the City: Ministries of Community Renewal* (Valley Forge, PA: Judson Press, 1999), 63.

19 Simpson, quoted in Carle and Decaro Jr., eds., *Signs of Hope in the City*, 63.

20. Ram Cnaan, quoted in Tennant, "Counting (Helping) Hands," 26.

Camus Finds the Exit

1. Jean-Paul Sartre, *No Exit and Three Other Plays* (New York: Vintage, 1989), 45.

2. Clark H. Pinnock, *Flame of Love: A Theology of the Holy Spirit* (Downers Grove, IL: InterVarsity, 1996), 141.

3. Acts 1:8.

4. Howard E. Mumma, *Albert Camus and the Minister* (Orleans, MA: Paraclete, 2000), quoted in James Sire, "Camus the Christian?" *Christianity Today* 44, no. 12 (October 23, 2000): 109, www.christianitytoday.com/ct/2000/012/39.12l.html.

The Sacrament of Belonging

1. Howard E. Mumma, *Albert Camus and the Minister* (Orleans, MA: Paraclete, 2000), quoted in James Sire, "Camus the Christian?" *Christianity Today* 44, no. 12 (October 23, 2000): 109, www.christianitytoday.com/ct/2000/012/39.12l.html.

2. Acts 2:38.

3. Albert Camus, *The Plague* (New York: Random House, 1947), 92.

4. Mumma, *Albert Camus and the Minister,* quoted in Sire, "Camus the Christian?"

5. Jesus said, "Whoever believes and is baptized will be saved, but whoever does not believe will be condemned" (Mark 16:16).

6. The Didache, in Maxwell Staniforth, ed., *Early Christian Writings,* rev. ed. (New York: Penguin, 1987), 194.

Weeping Willows

1. Clark H. Pinnock, *Flame of Love: A Theology of the Holy Spirit* (Downers Grove, IL: InterVarsity, 1996), 122.

2. 1 Corinthians 11:23-26.

3. John 6:35.

4. Justin Martyr, quoted in Robert Webber, *Ancient-Future Faith: Rethinking Evangelicalism for a Postmodern World* (Grand Rapids: Baker, 1999), 110-11.

Saving Time

1. Alexander Schmemann, *For the Life of the World: Sacraments and Orthodoxy* (Crestwood, NY: St. Vladimir's Seminary Press, 2002), 47.

2. Schmemann, *For the Life of the World,* 54.

Hope

1. Kurt Cobain, excerpt of suicide note, April 5, 1994.

2. Christopher Sandford, *Kurt Cobain* (New York: Carroll and Graf, 1995), 9, 333-34.

3. Kurt Cobain, *Journals* (New York: Riverhead Books, 2002), 5, 175, 189, 235.

4. William H. Frist, "Taking Our Stand Against HIV/AIDS," July 24, 2002, www.vanderbilt.edu/AnS/religious_studies/aidsafrica/theawakeproject.html.

5. 1 Corinthians 15:14,17,19-26.

What I Learned from Sean

1. John 17:20-21.

2. Gilbert Bilezikian, *Community 101* (Grand Rapids: Zondervan, 1997), 27.

3. Athanasian Creed, quoted in Kevin Giles, *What on Earth Is the Church: A Biblical and Theological Enquiry* (Downers Grove, IL: InterVarsity, 1995), 267.

4. Galatians 3:28.

5. Matthew 20:25,26.

Scraping Cosmonauts off the Ceiling

1. Alexander Schmemann, *For the Life of the World: Sacraments and Orthodoxy* (Crestwood, NY: St. Vladimir's Seminary Press, 2002), 118.

2. Psalm 29:2.

3. Revelation 4:11.

4. Revelation 5:9.

Saadia's Gift

1. 1 Peter 2:9-10.

2. A sample of the temple warning inscription and the English translation can be found at www.abu.nb.ca/Courses/NTIntro/InTest/JerTem.htm.

3. Ephesians 2:14,15.

4. Galatians 3:28.

5. Philemon 15-16.

6. Revelation 5:9-10.

Father Paneloux's Sermon

1. Albert Camus, *The Plague* (New York: Random House, 1947), 89-90.

2. Camus, *The Plague*, 194-97.

3. Matthew 8:14-15. Some have argued that John 11:4—where Jesus says of Lazarus's sickness "it is for God's glory"—shows that God gives us sickness so he can glorify himself. The point of the Lazarus story, however, is the defeat of sickness when Jesus raises him from the dead. God is glorified as Jesus defeats sickness.

4. Matthew 9:35-36.

5. James 5:14.

6. Camus, *The Plague*, 278.

7. Dionysius, quoted in Rodney Stark, *The Rise of Christianity* (Princeton, NJ: Princeton University Press, 1996), 82.

8. Richard Stearns, quoted in Nara Schoenberg, "World Vision Leader's Vision Is Fight Against AIDS," *Chicago Tribune,* May 15, 2003.

9. Mr. Sterns made these remarks to a group of potential donors in the spring of 2003. I was present at the meeting.

Politics as Shalom Making

1. Jim Wallis, *Who Speaks for God? An Alternative to the Religious Right—A New Politics of Compassion, Community, and Civility* (New York: Bantam Dell, 1996), ix.

2. Jeremiah 29:7.

3. Václav Havel, *The Art of the Impossible: Politics as Morality in Practice,* trans. Paul Wilson (New York: Fromm International, 1994), 101.

New Science and the New Community

1. The three theories are the theory of relativity, the theory of quantum physics, and chaos theory. See James Gleick, *Chaos: Making a New Science* (New York: Penguin, 1987), 6. For more on this idea, see Paul Davies, one of the world's leading science writers, who summarizes the revolution in his book *God and the New Physics* (New York: Touchstone, 1983).

2. Davies, *God and the New Physics,* vii.

3. Brian D. McLaren, *A New Kind of Christian: A Tale of Two Friends on a Spiritual Journey* (San Francisco: Jossey-Bass, 2001).

4. Margaret J. Wheatley, *Leadership and the New Science: Discovering Order in a Chaotic World* (San Francisco: Berrett-Koehler, 1999), 33.

5. Wheatley, *Leadership and the New Science,* 28.

6. 1 Corinthians 12:12.

7. Peter M. Senge, *The Fifth Discipline: Mastering the Five Practices of the Learning Organization* (New York: Doubleday, 1990), 68-69.

8. 1 Corinthians 12:26.

9. To explore this idea further, see Brian D. McLaren, *The Church on the Other Side: Doing Ministry in the Postmodern Matrix* (Grand Rapids: Zondervan, 2000); Peter Senge, *The Fifth Discipline;* and Edwin H. Friedman, *Generation to Generation: Family Process in Church and Synagogue* (New York: Guilford, 1985)

On Not Leaving It to the Hollow Men

1. Douglas Coupland, *Generation X: Tales for an Accelerated Culture* (London: Abacus, 1992), 26.

2. Luke 22:26.

3. See Ephesians 4:7-16.

4. See Acts 14:23.

5. Titus 1:5. See also 1 Timothy 5:17.

6. John Arquilla and David Ronfeldt, eds., *Networks and Netwars: The Future of Terror, Crime, and Militancy* (Arlington, VA: RAND, 2001), 6.

7. Bill Easum, *Leadership on the Other Side: No Rules, Just Clues* (Nashville: Abingdon, 2000), 13.

8. 1 Corinthians 12:21,27.

9. 1 Timothy 3:2-4,7.

10. Edwin H. Friedman, *Generation to Generation: Family Process in Church and Synagogue* (New York: Guilford, 1985), chap. 9.

11. Joel Garreau, "Point Men for a Revolution: Can the Marines Survive a Shift from Hierarchies to Networks?" *Washington Post* (March 6, 1999): 1.

12. Garreau, "Point Men for a Revolution," 1.

The People of the Lie

1. See Arthur Miller, *The Crucible* (New York: Penguin, 1982).

2. Matthew 18:15-17.

3. 1 Corinthians 5:1-2,4-5.

4. Jamie Satterfield, "Killer's Penalty Stiffened," *Knoxville News-Sentinel* (June 17, 2003): B-1.

5. John 10:12.

6. M. Scott Peck, *People of the Lie: The Hope for Healing Human Evil* (New York: Touchstone, 1985), 43.

7. Peck, *People of the Lie*, 77.

8. See Peck, *People of the Lie*, 77.

9. Peck, *People of the Lie*, 66.

10. Peck, *People of the Lie*, 66.

11. Galatians 6:1.

12. Peck, *People of the Lie*, 71.

13. 1 Corinthians 5:5.

Black Elk Still Speaks

1. See John G. Neihardt, *Black Elk Speaks* (Lincoln, NE: University of Nebraska Press, 2004).

2. Lynne White Jr., "The Historical Roots of Our Ecological Crisis," *Science* 155, no. 3767 (March 10, 1967): 1203-7.

3. James Watt, quoted in the *Washington Post,* May 24, 1981, www .skepticism.info/quotes/archives/christian_extremism/000226.shtml

4. See Brian D. McLaren, *A New Kind of Christian: A Tale of Two Friends on a Spiritual Journey* (San Francisco: Jossey-Bass, 2001).

5. Romans 8:21.

6. See Exodus 23:10-11 and Numbers 35:33-34.

7. Psalm 104:27-30.

8. Francis Schaeffer, *Pollution and the Death of Man: The Christian View of Ecology* (Wheaton, IL: Tyndale, 1970), 49-50.

9. 2 Peter 3:10.

10. Romans 8:21; Revelation 21:1,4.

11. Black Elk, quoted in Michael Steltenkamp, *Black Elk: Holy Man of the Oglala* (Norman, OK: University of Oklahoma Press, 1993), 83-84.

The Church and Other Religions

1. Rev. Jane Holmes Dixon, quoted in Associated Press, "Four Former Presidents Take Part in Prayer Service at Washington's National Cathedral," September 14, 2001, http://abclocal.go.com/wabc/news/ WABC_091401_ceremony.html.

2. Harold A. Netland, *Encountering Religious Pluralism: The Challenge to Christian Faith and Mission* (Downers Grove, IL: InterVarsity, 2001), 9-11.

3. Diana L. Eck, "True Liberty Cherishes Differences," *Los Angeles Times,* July 5, 1992.

4. Diana L. Eck, "The Challenge of Pluralism," *Neiman Reports,* vol. 47, no. 2 (Summer 1993).

5. Alexandrea Frean, "Blair Studies Koran in Multifaith Campaign," *The Times*, March 10, 2000.

6. Franklin Graham, quoted in "Interview with Gordon Robertson," *The 700 Club* (2004), www.cbn.com/700club/profiles/franklin_graham.asp. Graham later explained his remark, saying he doesn't believe that Muslim people are evil; rather, it's the evil done in the name of any religion that's lamentable. However, he didn't back down from his assertion that Islam is a religion that has historically persecuted and sought to eliminate non-Muslims.

7. Quoted in Alan Cooperman, "Anti-Muslim Remarks Stir Tempest," *Washington Post*, June 20, 2002, www.washingtonpost.com/ac2/wp-dyn/A14499-2002Jun19?language=printer.

8. Quoted in Deborah Caldwell, "How Islam Bashing Got Cool," www.beliefnet.com/story/110/story_11074.html.

9. William L. Shirer, *Gandhi*, performed by Larry McKeever, (Newport Beach, CA: Books on Tape, 1998), audiocassette.

10. Shirer, *Ghandi*.

11. Shirer, *Ghandi*.

12. Martin Luther King, Jr., *The Autobiography of Martin Luther King, Jr.*, ed. Carson Clayborne (New York: Warner Books, 1998), 17.

13. King, *The Autobiography of Martin Luther King, Jr.*, 23-24.

14. King, *The Autobiography of Martin Luther King, Jr.*, 131.

15. King, *The Autobiography of Martin Luther King, Jr.*, 131.

16. Acts 10:2,4.

17. See Matthew 2:1-12.

18. See Acts 17:22-28.

19. N. Ross Reat and Edmund F. Perry, *A World Theology: The Central Spiritual Reality of Humankind* (Cambridge: Cambridge University Press, 1991).

20. Joshua 24:14.

21. Matthew 28:19.

22. 1 Corinthians 8:5-7.

23. John 14:6.

24. Acts 4:12.

Still Point in the Turning World

1. See Ephesians 2:19-22 and 1 Peter 2:5.

2. Henri J. M. Nouwen, *Clowning in Rome: Reflections on Solitude, Celibacy, Prayer and Contemplation* (Garden City, NY: Image Books, 1979), 37.

3. Colossians 3:17.

4. T. S. Eliot, "Burnt Norton" in *Four Quartets* (New York: Harcourt, Brace & World, 1971), 15. Quoted in Robert M. Hamma, *Landscapes of the Soul: A Spirituality of Place* (Notre Dame: Ave Maria Press, 1999), 45.

The Four Walls of My Freedom

1. Exodus 20:4.

2. See Exodus 26:1,31; 25:18,33; 28:33.

3. Exodus 31:1-5,6.

4. Genesis 1:27.

5. Madeleine L'Engle, *Walking on Water* (Colorado Springs: Shaw, 2002), 15.

6. Thomas Merton, *The Seven Storey Mountain: An Autobiography of Faith* (San Diego: Harcourt, 1999), 410.

7. Merton, *The Seven Storey Mountain,* 428.

One Church, Many Congregations

1. Garrison Keillor, *Lake Wobegon Days* (New York: Penguin, 1985), 105-6.

2. See John 17:20-23.

3. John 17:23.

4. See, for example, Acts 8:1; 13:1; 18:22; 20:17; Romans 16:1,3-4; 1 Corinthians 1:2; 16:19; Philippians 1:1; Colossians 4:15-16; 1 Thessalonians 1:1; Philemon 1-2; Revelation 2:1,8,12,18; 3:1,7,14.

Epilogue

1. Natalie Goldberg, *Writing Down the Bones: Freeing the Writer Within* (Boston: Shambhala, 1986), 13.

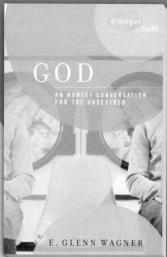
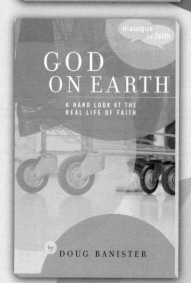
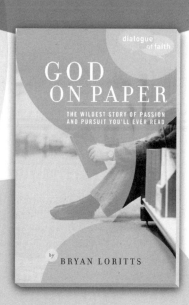

To learn more about WaterBrook Press and view
our catalog of products, log on to our Web site:
www.waterbrookpress.com

WATERBROOK
PRESS